i-Ready® Classroom
Mathematics

Grade 2 • Volume 1

Curriculum Associates

NOT FOR RESALE

Contents

Contents (continued)

UNIT 2

Numbers Within 100
Addition, Subtraction, Time, and Money

Numbers Within 1,000
Place Value, Addition, and Subtraction

UNIT 4

Length
Measurement, Addition and Subtraction, and Line Plots

UNIT 5

Shapes and Arrays
Partitioning and Tiling Shapes, Arrays, Evens and Odds

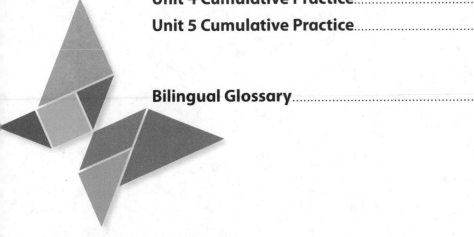

☑ SELF CHECK

Before starting this unit, check off the skills you know below. As you complete each lesson, see how many more skills you can check off!

I can . . .	Before	After
Count on to add and subtract.	☐	☐
Use fact families to add and subtract.	☐	☐
Make a ten to add and subtract.	☐	☐
Solve a one-step word problem.	☐	☐
Draw and find information from pictures and bar graphs.	☐	☐
Use addition and subtraction to solve a problem with more than one step.	☐	☐

Build Your Vocabulary

REVIEW

addend   addition equation
double   subtract
total

Math Vocabulary

Complete the sentences using what you know about each word.

Sentence Starter	What You Know
I think an **addend** is . . .	
I think an **addition equation** is . . .	
I think a **double** is . . .	
I think **subtract** means . . .	
I think the **total** is . . .	

Academic Vocabulary

Put a check next to the academic words you know.
Then use the words to complete the sentences.

☐ model   ☐ solve   ☐ explanation   ☐ purpose

1 Writing out math problems helps me .... them.

2 The .... of learning fact families is to learn how to add and subtract in my head.

3 My teacher's .... helped me understand the problem better.

4 Base-ten blocks can be used as a .... for counting by tens.

Mental Math Strategies for Addition

Dear Family,

This week your child is learning how to use different mental math strategies for addition.

Here are some addition strategies that your child will learn.

Count On

An addition problem can be solved by counting on. You can count from a number in a problem to find the total. This strategy will help your child find the number of objects in a group without counting each one.

To find 8 + 3, start with 8. Then count on 3, the other number in the problem. 8, . . . , 9, 10, 11. So, 8 + 3 = 11.

Doubles Plus 1

A doubles fact is an addition problem in which the two addends (the numbers being added) are the same, such as 8 + 8. A doubles plus 1 fact is an addition problem in which one of the addends is one more than the other, such as 8 + 9.

Find 8 + 9.	8 + 9
Think of 9 as 8 + 1.	8 + 8 + 1
Add the double, 8 + 8.	16
Add 1 to the **sum** of 16.	16 + 1 = 17
Give the answer for 8 + 9.	8 + 9 = 17

Make a Ten

Adding can be easier when one number is 10. By breaking apart a number, you can add to make 10, and then add the rest.

Find 6 + 8.

Think of 8 as 4 + 4.

Add 6 and 4 to make 10.

Add the other 4.

$$
\begin{array}{c}
6 \; + \; 8 \\
\diagup \; \diagdown \\
6 \; + 4 + 4 \\
\diagdown \diagup \; \diagdown \\
10 \quad + 4 \\
\diagdown \; \diagup \\
14
\end{array}
$$

> Adding 10 + 4 is an easier problem to solve mentally: 10 + 4 = 14, so 6 + 8 = 14.

Invite your child to share what he or she knows about making a ten by doing the following activity together.

ACTIVITY MAKING A TEN

Do this activity with your child to practice adding using mental math strategies.

- Begin by holding up 6 fingers. Ask your child to add 9 to that number.

- Have your child add the numbers by "making a 10" and using your fingers to model the process. (For example, your child might start by adding 4 and putting the rest of your fingers up, and then adding 5 of his or her own fingers to model adding 9.)

- Ask your child questions such as: *If I hold up 8 fingers, how can I add 7 by making a ten?*

- Repeat with other numbers of fingers, playing for about 5 minutes.

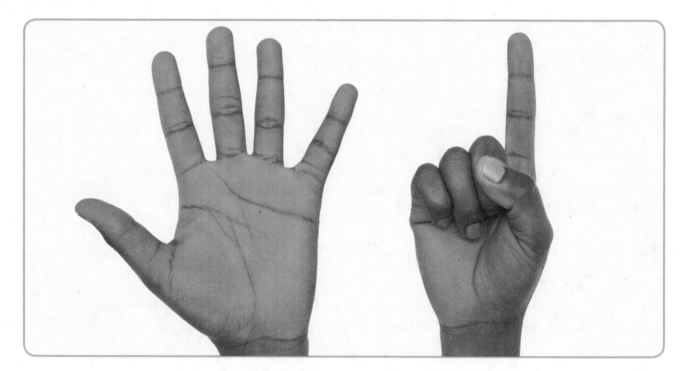

Explore Using Mental Math Strategies for Addition

In this lesson, you will use different strategies to add numbers in your head. Use what you know to try to solve the problem below.

Learning Target
• Fluently add and subtract within 20 using mental strategies. By end of Grade 2, know from memory all sums of two one-digit numbers.

SMP 1, 2, 3, 4, 5, 6, 7, 8

> **There are 8 children on the playground. Then 4 more children join them. How many children in all are on the playground?**

TRY IT

 **Math Toolkit**
• counters
• 10-frames

DISCUSS IT

Ask your partner: How did you get started?

Tell your partner: At first, I thought . . .

CONNECT IT

1 LOOK BACK

How many children in all are on the playground? ....

2 LOOK AHEAD

Numbers you **add** are called addends. You can add numbers in different ways. Choose a way that you think works best. Making a ten is one way to add numbers with a **sum** greater than 10.

Think about 8 + 5.

Break apart the 5. Add to 8 to make 10.

a. What do you need to add to 8 to make 10? ....

b. How much more do you need to add? ....

c. Complete each **equation** with the **unknown number** to show how to make a ten to add 8 + 5.

8 + ... = 10

10 + ... = 13

So, 8 + 5 = ...

3 REFLECT

How did you know how many more to add after you made 10?

....

Prepare for Using Mental Math Strategies for Addition

1 Think about what you know about different ways to add. Fill in each box. Use words, numbers, and pictures. Show as many ideas as you can.

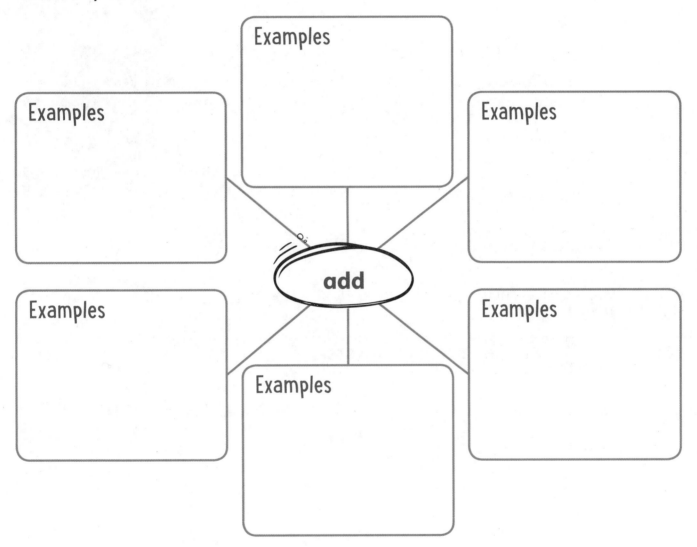

Examples

Examples

Examples

Examples

Examples

Examples

add

2 Explain how you would add 8 + 7.

3 Solve the problem. Show your work.

There are 7 goats at the petting zoo. Then 6 more goats are brought to the petting zoo. How many goats in all are at the petting zoo?

Solution ....

4 Check your answer. Show your work.

Develop Adding by Counting On and Making a Ten

Read and try to solve the problem below.

> **Khalid reads 9 books during June. Then he reads 3 more books in July. How many books does Khalid read in both months?**

TRY IT

 **Math Toolkit**
- counters
- connecting cubes

DISCUSS IT

Ask your partner: Do you agree with me? Why or why not?

Tell your partner: I disagree with this part because . . .

Explore different ways to understand using strategies for solving addition problems in your head.

> **Khalid reads 9 books during June. Then he reads 3 more books in July. How many books does Khalid read in both months?**

PICTURE IT
You can count on to add.

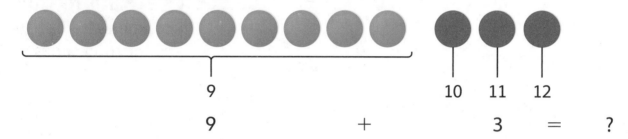

9

9 + 3 = ?

MODEL IT
You can make a ten to add.

9 + 3 = ?
9 + 1 + 2 = ?
10 + 2 = ?

MODEL IT
You can show making a ten to add on an **open number line**.

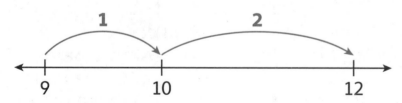

CONNECT IT

Now you will use the problem from the previous page to help you understand how to add by counting on and making a ten.

1 Look at **Picture It**. What number do you get after you count on:

1 more than 9? ....

2 more than 9? ....

3 more than 9? ....

2 Look at the **Model Its**.

What is 10 + 2? ....

3 What is 9 + 3? ....

4 Why is 9 + 3 the same as 10 + 2?

5 How many books does Khalid read in both months? ....

6 REFLECT

Look back at your **Try It**, strategies by classmates, and **Picture It** and **Model Its**. Which models or strategies do you like best for adding in your head? Explain.

....

....

....

APPLY IT

Use what you just learned to solve these problems.

7 Tom has 3 blue shirts and 8 red shirts. How many shirts does he have in all? Show how you found your answer.

8 Show how you can make a ten to help you add 7 + 6.

9 To find 7 + 4 = ? Dan counts on. He shows how he counts on in this table. What does he do wrong?

7	8	9	10	11
/	/	/	/	

Lesson 1 Mental Math Strategies for Addition

Practice Adding by Counting On or Making a Ten

Study the Example showing how to make a ten to add.
Then solve problems 1–6.

EXAMPLE

Find 8 + 7.

8 + 7 = ?
8 + **2** + ?

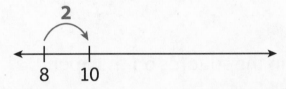

The partners 8 and 2 make 10.

8 + 7 = ?
8 + 2 + **5**

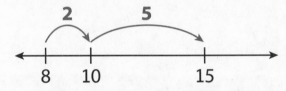

Add 5, the other partner of 7.

So, 8 + 7 = 15.

---

1   Fill in the squares to find 9 + 4.

9 + 4 = ?
9 + ☐ + ☐

So, 9 + 4 = ...

2   Look at the open number line in problem 1. How would you change the numbers to show 9 + 5?

3 Make a ten to add. Fill in the squares on the open number line to show $9 + 6 = 15$.

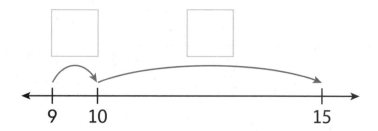

4 Make a ten to add. Fill in the squares on the open number line to find $8 + 5$.

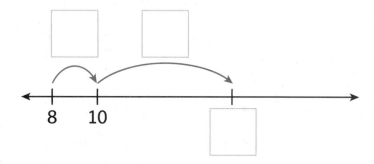

$8 + 5 =$ ....

5 Count on to find $9 + 7$. Fill in the blanks.

6 Find $9 + 2$. Show how you found your answer. Count on or use the make a ten strategy. Explain why you chose that strategy.

Develop Using Doubles and Doubles Plus 1

Read and try to solve the problem below.

> Lara has 8 blue marbles and 9 red marbles.
> How many marbles does she have?

TRY IT

 Math Toolkit
- counters
- number lines

DISCUSS IT

Ask your partner: Can you explain that again?

Tell your partner: The strategy I used to find the answer was . . .

Explore different ways to understand using more strategies for solving addition problems in your head.

Lara has 8 blue marbles and 9 red marbles. How many marbles does she have?

PICTURE IT

You can use pictures to show doubles plus 1 more.

Find the double.

8 + 8 = ?

Find one more.

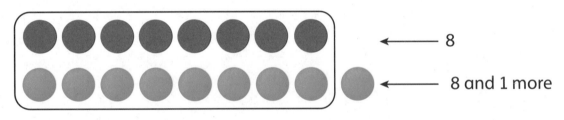

⟵ 8

⟵ 8 and 1 more

8 + 8 + 1 = ?

MODEL IT

You can break apart numbers to show doubles plus 1.

Find the total.

8 + 9 = ?
8 + 8 + 1 = ?

CONNECT IT

Now you will use the problem from the previous page to help you understand how to add using doubles and doubles plus 1.

1 Why do you think 8 + 8 is called a double?

2 What is 8 + 8? ....

3 How does knowing 8 + 8 help you find 8 + 9?

4 How many marbles does Lara have? ....

5 How would you use a doubles fact to find 5 + 6?

6 REFLECT

Look back at your **Try It**, strategies by classmates, and **Picture It** and **Model It**. Which models or strategies do you like best for solving a doubles plus 1 fact? Explain.

....

....

....

Lesson 1 Mental Math Strategies for Addition   **17**

APPLY IT

Use what you just learned to solve these problems.

7 $9 + 9 = 18$. How can you use this to solve $9 + 10$?

8 Maria earns 8 dollars planting flowers. Then she earns 7 dollars feeding pets. How much does she earn in all?

Write an equation that uses doubles plus 1 to solve the problem. Show your work.

9 Kelly said that she found $3 + 4$ by finding $4 + 4 - 1$. Do you think that she is correct? Explain.

Practice Using Doubles and Doubles Plus 1

Study the Example showing how to add using doubles plus 1. Then solve problems 1–5.

EXAMPLE

David has 7 stickers with hearts and 8 stickers with stars. How many stickers does David have in all?

$7 + 8 = ?$

Use doubles.

Then add 1 more.

$7 + 7 + 1 = 15$

$7 + 8 = 15$

David has 15 stickers in all.

1 Complete these doubles facts.

$4 + 4 =$ .... $5 + 5 =$ ....

$6 + 6 =$ .... $7 + 7 =$ ....

$8 + 8 =$ .... $9 + 9 =$ ....

2 Which of the doubles facts above would you use to solve $8 + 9$? Explain.

3 Use doubles plus 1 to solve this problem.

Cory finds 6 shells at the beach. Later, he finds 5 more shells. How many shells does he find in all?

Ⓐ 10

Ⓑ 11

Ⓒ 12

Ⓓ 13

4 Write the double that you would use to solve each problem. Then solve it.

a. 4 + 5 = ?

Use the double .... + ...

4 + 5 = ...

b. 7 + 6 = ?

Use the double .... + ...

7 + 6 = ...

c. 5 + 6 = ?

Use the double .... + ...

5 + 6 = ...

5 James wants to solve 6 + 7. He used 7 + 7 and 1 more. Did James get the correct answer? Explain.

Complete the Example below. Then solve problems 1–3.

EXAMPLE

Tina plays basketball 8 hours in one week. The next week, she plays basketball for 6 hours. How many hours does she play in both weeks?

Find $8 + 6$. You can break apart numbers to make a ten.

Break apart 8. $8 + 6$

$4 + 4$

$4 + 6 = 10$

Add 4 more. $10 + 4 = 14$

$8 + 6 = 14$

Break apart 6. $8 + 6$

$2 + 4$

$8 + 2 = 10$

Add 4 more. $10 + 4 = 14$

$8 + 6 = 14$

Solution ....

APPLY IT

1 Elon takes 7 pictures at home. Then he takes 5 more pictures at school. How many pictures does Elon take in all? Show your work.

You can think of 7 as 5 and 2.

Solution ....

2 Find 8 + 3 by counting on. Show your work.

Which addend will you start with?

Solution ....

3 What is 8 + 9?

Ⓐ 16

Ⓑ 17

Ⓒ 18

Ⓓ 19

You might want to use a double.

Lydia chose Ⓓ as the correct answer.
How did Lydia get her answer?

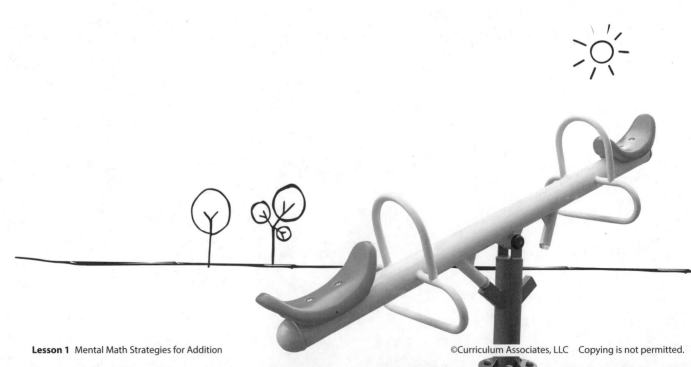

Practice Using Mental Math Strategies for Addition

1 Karen buys 5 red apples and 6 yellow apples. How many apples does she buy in all? Show your work.

Can a double plus 1 help?

Solution ....

2 Brad builds a tower with 8 blocks. Then he puts 7 more blocks on his tower. How many blocks are on his tower now? Show your work.

$7 + 7 = 14$

Solution ....

3 Alicia has 10 books to return to the library. Her sister has 9 books to return. How many books do the girls have to return to the library in all? Show your work.

What do you need to find?

Solution ....

4 Find 6 + 7. Tell if you can use each of these to solve the problem.

	Yes	No
6 + 6 + 1	Ⓐ	Ⓑ
7 + 7 + 1	Ⓒ	Ⓓ
7 + 3 + 3	Ⓔ	Ⓕ
10 + 4	Ⓖ	Ⓗ

What strategies could you use to find the answer?

5 Raul has a stack of 10 pennies. He makes another stack of 10 pennies. How many pennies are in the stacks in all? Show your work.

Think about doubles facts.

Solution

6 What is 4 + 8?

Ⓐ 14   Ⓑ 13

Ⓒ 12   Ⓓ 11

You can count on or make a ten to solve this problem!

Sam chose Ⓓ as the correct answer.

How did Sam get his answer?

Refine Using Mental Math Strategies for Addition

APPLY IT

Solve the problems.

1 Emma puts 9 berries on her cereal. Then she puts 2 more berries on her cereal. How many berries are on her cereal now?

Ⓐ 7　　　　　　　　　Ⓑ 9

Ⓒ 10　　　　　　　　Ⓓ 11

2 Max puts 9 quarters and 8 dimes in his piggy bank. How many coins in all does he put in his piggy bank? Which equations could you use to solve the problem?

Ⓐ $1 + 9 + 9 = ?$

Ⓑ $8 + 8 + 1 = ?$

Ⓒ $9 + 9 + 1 = ?$

Ⓓ $9 + 1 + 7 = ?$

Ⓔ $1 + 8 + 8 = ?$

3 Find $5 + 6$. Tell if you can use each equation to solve the problem.

	Yes	No
$1 + 6 + 6 = ?$	Ⓐ	Ⓑ
$5 + 5 + 1 = ?$	Ⓒ	Ⓓ
$6 + 4 + 1 = ?$	Ⓔ	Ⓕ
$6 + 6 + 1 = ?$	Ⓖ	Ⓗ

4 Greta and Chuck each find $5 + 7$ by making a ten.

Greta	Chuck
Break apart 5. $5 + 7$	Break apart 7. $5 + 7$
$2 + 3$	$5 + 2$
$7 + 3 = 10$	$5 + 5 = 10$
Add 2 more. $10 + 2 = 12$	Add 2 more. $10 + 2 = 12$
$7 + 5 = 12$	$7 + 5 = 12$

Do they both make a ten correctly? Explain.

5 Ming finds $9 + 8$. See her work at the right. What does she do wrong? What is the correct answer?

$$9 + 1 = 10$$
$$10 + 8 = 18$$
$$9 + 8 = 18$$

6 MATH JOURNAL

What are two ways you can solve $8 + 9$? Explain.

 SELF CHECK Go back to the Unit 1 Opener and see what you can check off.

Mental Math Strategies for Subtraction

Dear Family,

This week your child is learning how to use different mental math strategies for subtraction.

Here are some subtraction strategies that your child will learn.

Count On

A subtraction problem can be solved by counting on. What is $15 - 9$? Your child can think of $15 - 9 = ?$ as $9 + ? = 15$. Count on from 9 to 15. 9, . . . 10, 11, 12, 13, 14, 15

You counted on 6 numbers. That means $9 + 6 = 15$, so $15 - 9 = 6$.

Make a Ten

The "make a ten" strategy can be modeled with an open number line (a number line not drawn to scale, with only the numbers important to the problem labeled).

$15 - 9 = ?$	Think of 9 as **5** + **4**.
$15 - 5 = 10$	Subtract **5** to get to 10.
$10 - 4 = 6$	Then subtract the remaining **4**.

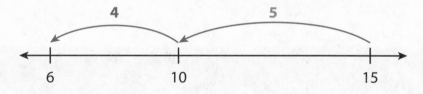

$15 - 9 = 6$

Use Fact Families

A **fact family** is a group of related equations that use the same numbers but in a different order.

$$9 + 6 = 15 \qquad 6 + 9 = 15 \qquad 15 - 9 = 6 \qquad 15 - 6 = 9$$

$15 - 9 = ?$ is the same as $9 + ? = 15$, and if your child knows that $9 + 6 = 15$, then he or she knows that $15 - 9 = 6$.

Invite your child to share what he or she knows about using fact families by doing the following activity together.

ACTIVITY FACT FAMILIES

Do this activity with your child to explore using mental math strategies for subtraction.

Work with your child to create fact family cards by cutting out the facts below and coloring the backs or by writing the facts on index cards. Then use the cards for the activity.

- Each player chooses one of the single-number cards (14 or 17) and places it faceup in front of him or her. Shuffle the fact cards. Place them facedown in 2 rows with 4 cards in each row.

- Players take turns flipping over two cards.

  - If either of the cards are not in the same fact family as the player's number card, then put them both back facedown.

  - If both of the cards are in the same fact family as the number card, then the player keeps the cards.

- The first player to find the 4 cards that make a family that goes with his or her number card wins.

$8 + 6 = 14$	$6 + 8 = 14$	$14 - 8 = 6$
$14 - 6 = 8$	$9 + 8 = 17$	$8 + 9 = 17$
$17 - 9 = 8$	$17 - 8 = 9$	14 17

Explore Using Mental Math Strategies for Subtraction

In this lesson you will use different strategies to subtract numbers in your head. Use what you know to try to solve the problem below.

Learning Target
• Fluently add and subtract within 20 using mental strategies. By end of Grade 2, know from memory all sums of two one-digit numbers.

SMP 1, 2, 3, 4, 5, 6, 7, 8

> **Chen has 14 stamps. He uses 6 of them to mail letters. How many stamps does Chen have left?**

TRY IT

 **Math Toolkit**
• counters
• 10-frames

DISCUSS IT

Ask your partner: Do you agree with me? Why or why not?

Tell your partner: I am not sure how to find the answer because . . .

CONNECT IT

1 **LOOK BACK**

How many stamps does Chen have left? ....

2 **LOOK AHEAD**

You can subtract numbers in different ways. Making a ten is one way to subtract from teen numbers.

Think about 14 − 5. Break apart the 5. Show how to subtract from 14 to make 10.

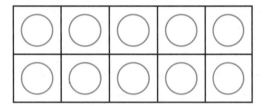 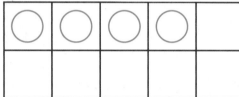

a. What do you need to subtract from 14 to make 10?

....

b. How much more do you need to subtract? ....

3 **REFLECT**

Why is subtracting 4 and then subtracting 1 the same as subtracting 5?

....

....

....

Prepare for Using Mental Math Strategies for Subtraction

1 Think about what you know about different ways to subtract. Fill in each box. Use words, numbers, and pictures. Show as many ideas as you can.

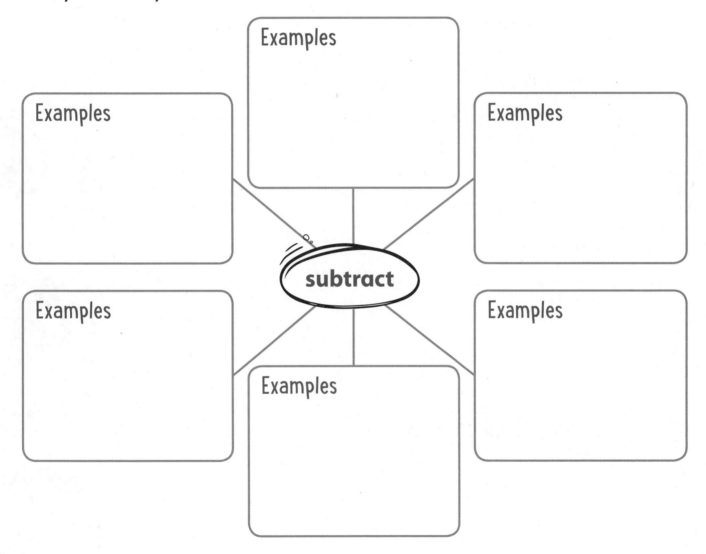

Examples

Examples

Examples

Examples

Examples

Examples

subtract

2 Explain how you would subtract 11 − 7.

3 Solve the problem. Show your work.

Parnell has 12 stickers. He gives 7 of them to friends. How many stickers does Parnell have left?

Solution ....

4 Check your answer. Show your work.

Develop Counting On and Making a Ten to Subtract

Read and try to solve the problem below.

> Sarah buys 11 balloons for her party. During the party, she gives away 8 of the balloons. How many balloons does Sarah have left?

TRY IT

 Math Toolkit
- counters
- 10-frames

DISCUSS IT

Ask your partner: Why did you choose that strategy?

Tell your partner: A model I used was . . . It helped me . . .

Explore different ways to understand solving subtraction problems in your head.

> **Sarah buys 11 balloons for her party. During the party, she gives away 8 of the balloons. How many balloons does Sarah have left?**

MODEL IT

You can count on to subtract.

You can find $11 - 8 = ?$ by finding $8 + ? = 11$.

Start at 8 in the table. Count on until you reach 11.

1	2	3	4	5	6	7	8	9	10
11	12	13	14	15	16	17	18	19	20

MODEL IT

You can make a ten to subtract.

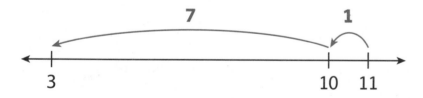

Subtract 1 to make a ten. $11 - 1 = 10$

Subtract 7 more to subtract 8 in all.

$10 - 7 = ?$

CONNECT IT

Now you will use the problem from the previous page to help you understand how to count on or make a ten to subtract.

1 Use the first **Model It** on the previous page. What number do you get after you count on:

1 more than 8? ....

2 more than 8? ....

3 more than 8? ....

2 Complete the equations.

8 + ... = 11   11 − 8 = ...

3 Use the second **Model It** on the previous page. Complete the equations.

11 − 1 = ...

10 − 7 = ...   So, 11 − 8 = ...

4 How many balloons does Sarah have left? ....

5 REFLECT

Look back at your **Try It**, strategies by classmates, and **Model Its**. Which models or strategies do you like best for subtracting in your head? Explain.

....

....

APPLY IT

Use what you just learned to solve these problems.

6 Show how to find $12 - 7 = ?$ by counting on.

7 Find $14 - 7$ by making a ten using equations.

Solution ....

8 Use your answer from problem 7 to fill in the squares on the open number line.

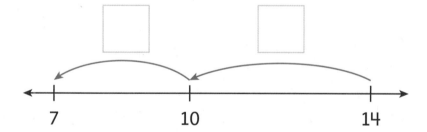

Practice Counting On and Making a Ten to Subtract

Study how the Example shows counting on to subtract in your head. Then solve problems 1–6.

EXAMPLE

$13 - 9 = ?$

Think of it as $9 + ? = 13$.

Count on to get from 9 to 13.

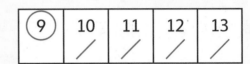

The marks show how many you counted on.

Solve the addition problem. $9 + 4 = 13$

Solve the subtraction problem. $13 - 9 = 4$

---

1 Fill in the blanks in each equation.

$9 - 4 = ?$ is the same as .... $+ ? = $ ....

$8 - 3 = ?$ is the same as .... $+ ? = $ ....

$11 - 7 = ?$ is the same as .... $+ ? = $ ....

$15 - 8 = ?$ is the same as .... $+ ? = $ ....

2 Complete each addition fact to solve the subtraction equation.

$4 + $ .... $= 9$, so $9 - 4 = $ ....

$3 + $ .... $= 8$, so $8 - 3 = $ ....

$7 + $ .... $= 11$, so $11 - 7 = $ ....

$8 + $ .... $= 15$, so $15 - 8 = $ ....

3 Make a ten to subtract. Fill in the squares on the open number line to show $12 - 4 = 8$.

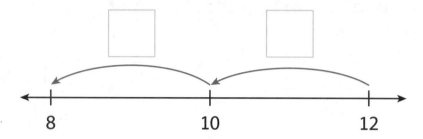

8   10   12

4 Complete the equations.

$12 - \boxed{} = 10$ $16 - \boxed{} = 10$

$13 - \boxed{} = 10$ $15 - \boxed{} = 10$

5 Fill in the squares to find $15 - 9$.

$15 - 9 = ?$

$15 - 9 = \boxed{}$

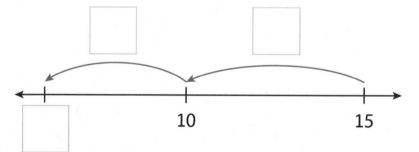

10   15

6 Jan circled the problems that she cannot solve in her head by making a ten.

$14 - 7$ $\boxed{8 - 2}$ $12 - 8$
      $\boxed{9 - 4}$ $15 - 6$

Look at all of the problems. Why does Jan not make a ten to solve the circled problems?

Develop Using Fact Families to Help Subtract

Read and try to solve the problem below.

> There are 15 birds swimming in a pond. Then
> 9 birds fly away. How many birds are left?

TRY IT

 **Math Toolkit**
- number chart 1–20
- number lines

DISCUSS IT

Ask your partner: How did you get started?

Tell your partner: I knew . . . so I . . .

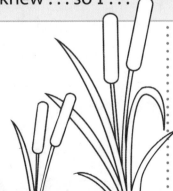

Explore another way to understand solving subtraction problems in your head.

> **There are 15 birds swimming in a pond. Then 9 birds fly away. How many birds are left?**

MODEL IT

Use a fact family to help solve the problem.

Find the **difference 15 − 9**.

Use the number bond to write a **fact family**.

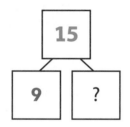

9 + ? = 15   15 − 9 = ?

? + 9 = 15   15 − ? = 9

CONNECT IT

Now you will use the problem from the previous page to help you understand how to use a fact family to subtract.

1 Look at **Model It**. Complete the number bond.

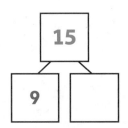

2 Use the number bond in problem 1 to complete the four facts for this fact family.

$9 +$ .... $= 15$ $15 - 9 =$ ....

.... $+ 9 = 15$ $15 -$ .... $= 9$

3 How many birds are left in the pond? ....

4 Use this number bond to complete another fact family.

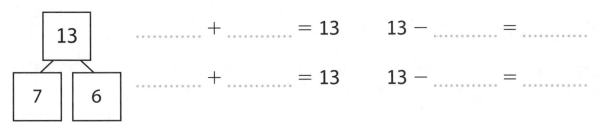

.... $+$ .... $= 13$ $13 -$ .... $=$ ....

.... $+$ .... $= 13$ $13 -$ .... $=$ ....

5 REFLECT

Look back at your **Try It**, strategies by classmates, and **Model It**. Which models or strategies do you like best for solving subtraction problems in your head? Explain.

....

....

....

APPLY IT

Use what you just learned to solve these problems.

6 Tia says that the equations below belong to the same fact family because they both have 5 and 8. Do you agree? Explain.

$5 + 8 = 13$ $\qquad\qquad$ $8 - 5 = 3$

7 Fill in the blanks in the equation.

$14 - 9 = ?$ is the same as .... $+ ? =$ ....

8 Fill in the number bond to find $14 - 9$.

9 How does picturing a number bond help you find $14 - 9$ in your head?

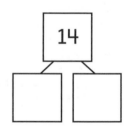

10 Which equations are in the fact family with $10 - 2 = 8$?

Ⓐ $8 + 2 = 10$

Ⓑ $10 - 8 = 2$

Ⓒ $10 + 2 = 12$

Ⓓ $12 - 8 = 4$

Ⓔ $2 + 8 = 10$

Practice Using Fact Families to Help Subtract

**Study the Example showing how adding helps you subtract.
Then solve problems 1–6.**

EXAMPLE

Solve 9 − 5.

Make a number bond.

```
     ┌─────┐
     │  9  │
     └─────┘
      ╱   ╲
  ┌─────┐ ┌─────┐
  │  5  │ │  ?  │
  └─────┘ └─────┘
```

Write an addition problem. Solve.

$$5 + ? = 9$$
$$5 + 4 = 9$$

Then solve the subtraction.

$$9 - 5 = 4$$

---

1 Complete the number bond to show 15 − 6 = ?.

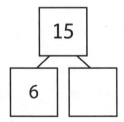

2 Write an addition equation for the number bond in problem 1. Then complete the subtraction equation.

.... + ... = ...

15 − 6 = ...

3 Complete the number bond. Write four equations.

.... + ... = 13   13 − .... = ...

13 = ... + ... = 13 − ....

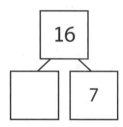

4 Complete the number bond to show 16 − 7 = ?.

5 Write the fact family for the number bond in problem 4.

.... + ... = ... + ... = ...

.... − .... = ... − .... = ...

6 Jose bakes 12 muffins. He gives 9 muffins to his friends. How many muffins does Jose have left?

Write a subtraction equation for the problem. Then write and solve a related addition equation. Use the addition equation to solve the subtraction equation.

.... − .... = ?

.... + ... = ...

So, ... − .... = ...

Jose has .... muffins left.

Refine Using Mental Math Strategies for Subtraction

Complete the Example below. Then solve problems 1–3.

EXAMPLE

Kendra has some strawberries. She eats 5 of them. Now she has 8 strawberries. How many strawberries did Kendra start with?

Write an equation with an unknown number. You can show the numbers in a number bond.

$? - 5 = 8$
Kendra eats 5 strawberries.
Then she has 8 strawberries.
Add $8 + 5$ to find the unknown number that she started with.
$8 + 5 = 13$. So, $13 - 5 = 8$.

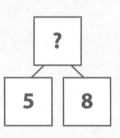

Solution ....

APPLY IT

1 Greg has 18 dollars. He spends 9 dollars on a game. How much money does Greg have left? Show your work.

Can making a ten help?

Solution ....

2 Find 12 − 8 by counting on. Show your work.

Which number will you count on from?

Solution ....

3 Which equations would be in the fact family for the number bond?

Ⓐ 12 = 7 + 5

Ⓑ 19 = 12 + 7

Ⓒ 7 = 12 − 5

Ⓓ 12 = 5 + 7

Ⓔ 5 = 12 − 7

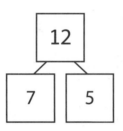

What do you know about all fact families?

Lily chose Ⓑ as the correct answer. How did she get that answer?

Practice Using Mental Math Strategies for Subtraction

1 Eli buys 12 oranges. He uses 7 of them to make a fruit salad. How many oranges does he have left? Show your work.

How can making a ten help?

Solution ....

2 Leti has some stickers. She gives 10 stickers to her brother. Leti has 10 stickers left. How many stickers did Leti have to begin with? Show your work.

Can you add to subtract?

Solution ....

3 Sonia has 15 toys. She puts 8 of them on a shelf. How many does she have left?

Could you use the equation to solve this problem? Choose *Yes* or *No* for each equation.

Can you solve the problem by using related facts in the same fact family?

	Yes	No
? + 8 = 15	Ⓐ	Ⓑ
15 + 8 = ?	Ⓒ	Ⓓ
15 − 8 = ?	Ⓔ	Ⓕ
8 + 15 = ?	Ⓖ	Ⓗ

4 What is 13 − 9?

Ⓐ 3

Ⓑ 4

Ⓒ 5

Ⓓ 10

You can count on or make a ten to solve this problem!

David chose Ⓒ as the correct answer.

How did David get his answer?

Refine Using Mental Math Strategies for Subtraction

APPLY IT
Solve the problems.

1 Javier has 12 eggs. He cooks 3 eggs for breakfast. How many eggs does Javier have left?

Ⓐ 15

Ⓑ 10

Ⓒ 9

Ⓓ 5

2 Which equations are in the fact family for this number bond?

Ⓐ $7 + 6 = 13$

Ⓑ $13 + 7 = 20$

Ⓒ $13 - 7 = 6$

Ⓓ $6 + 7 = 13$

Ⓔ $13 - 6 = 7$

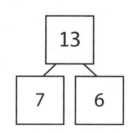

3 Could you make a ten to solve the problem? Choose *Yes* or *No* for each problem.

	Yes	No
$14 - 7$	Ⓐ	Ⓑ
$10 - 2$	Ⓒ	Ⓓ
$9 - 3$	Ⓔ	Ⓕ
$12 - 4$	Ⓖ	Ⓗ

4 Solve 12 − 5 = ? by using a related addition fact. Show how you solved the problem.

Solution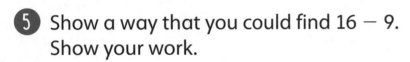

5 Show a way that you could find 16 − 9.
Show your work.

Solution ....

6 MATH JOURNAL

What are two ways you can find 17 − 8? Explain.

 SELF CHECK Go back to the Unit 1 Opener and see what you can check off.

Solve One-Step Word Problems

Dear Family,

This week your child is learning different ways to solve one-step word problems using addition or subtraction.

Consider the following word problem below.

Alex has 13 carrot sticks. He eats 5 carrot sticks. How many carrot sticks does he have left?

You can model this problem in many different ways.

You can write what you know and what you do not know.	**You can use a number bond.**
Total carrot sticks: 13 Carrot sticks eaten: 5 Carrot sticks left: ?	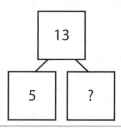

You can use a bar model (also called a tape diagram).

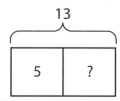

Each of these models will help you write all the facts of the fact family.

$$13 - 5 = ? \qquad 13 - ? = 5 \qquad 5 + ? = 13 \qquad ? + 5 = 13$$

You can solve to find that Alex has 8 carrot sticks left.

Invite your child to share what he or she knows about solving one-step word problems by doing the following activity together.

ACTIVITY SOLVING ONE-STEP WORD PROBLEMS

Do this activity with your child to explore solving one-step word problems.

Materials 20 small objects (pennies, buttons, bite-sized crackers), a cup or other container

- Place 9 pennies in one cup and 6 pennies on the table.

- Ask your child the four questions below. Each time, give one equation that could be used to solve the problem (provided in parentheses). Then have your child give all the related equations in the same fact family. (The equations in the fact family are given below the question.)

  1. How many coins are there in all? $(9 + 6 = 15)$

  2. How many more pennies are in the cup than on the table? $(9 - 6 = 3)$

  3. If I take away 2 pennies from the cup, how many pennies will be left in the cup? $(9 - 2 = 7)$

  4. How many pennies will I need to put on the table to have 10 pennies on the table? $(10 - 6 = 4)$

- Repeat with a different number of pennies in the cup and on the table.

Answers:
1. $9 + 6 = 15; 6 + 9 = 15; 15 - 9 = 6; 15 - 6 = 9$
2. $9 - 6 = 3; 9 - 3 = 6; 3 + 6 = 9; 6 + 3 = 9$
3. $9 - 2 = 7; 9 - 7 = 2; 2 + 7 = 9; 7 + 2 = 9$
4. $10 - 6 = 4; 10 - 4 = 6; 4 + 6 = 10; 6 + 4 = 10$

Explore Solving One-Step Word Problems

You have used different strategies to add and subtract. Use what you know to try to solve the problem below.

> **Seth has 9 grapes. His dad gives him some more grapes. Now Seth has 15 grapes. How many grapes did Seth's dad give him?**

TRY IT

 Math Toolkit

• counters
• 10-frames

DISCUSS IT

Ask your partner: Can you explain that again?

Tell your partner: I agree with you about … because …

CONNECT IT

1 LOOK BACK

How many grapes did Seth's dad give him? ....

2 LOOK AHEAD

a. You can use models to show the problem on the previous page. Fill in the unknown numbers in the bar model and the number bond.

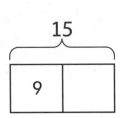

b. The **?** and the **equal sign (=)** can be in different places in the models and equations. Write the unknown number in each equation.

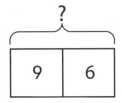 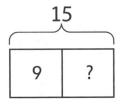 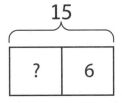

.... $= 9 + 6$ $15 = 9 +$ .... $15 =$ .... $+ 6$

3 REFLECT

Look at one of the equations you wrote. How does the equation show the problem?

....

....

....

Prepare for Solving One-Step Word Problems

1 Think about what you know about equations. Fill in each box. Use words, numbers, and pictures. Show as many ideas as you can.

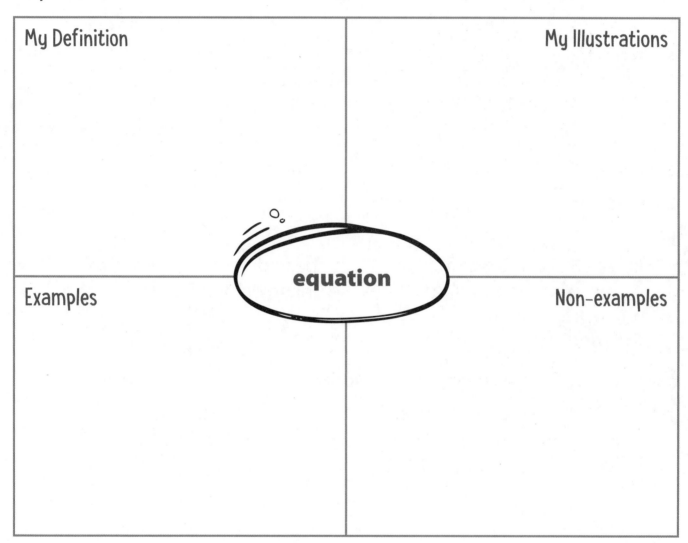

My Definition	My Illustrations

equation

Examples	Non-examples

2 Why do the equations 7 + ? = 15 and 15 − ? = 7 have the same solution?

3 Solve the problem. Show your work.

Fola has 8 berries. Her dad gives her some more berries. Now Fola has 13 berries. How many berries did Fola's dad give her?

Solution ....

4 Check your answer. Show your work.

Develop Solving Take-Apart Word Problems

Read and try to solve the problem below.

> There are 15 players on a team.
> There are 7 girls. The rest of the players
> are boys. How many boys are on the team?

TRY IT

 Math Toolkit
- counters
- ten frames
- blank bar models

DISCUSS IT

Ask your partner:
Why did you choose
that strategy?

Tell your partner: I
am not sure how to
find the answer
because . . .

Explore different ways to understand solving word problems.

> There are 15 players on a team. There are 7 girls. The rest of the players are boys. How many boys are on the team?

PICTURE IT
You can draw a picture.

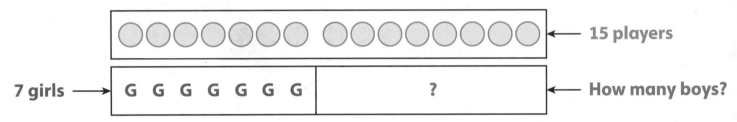

7 girls → | G G G G G G G | ? | ← How many boys?

← 15 players

MODEL IT
You can use words and numbers in a bar model.

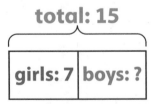

total: 15

| girls: 7 | boys: ? |

CONNECT IT

Now you will use the problem from the previous page to help you understand how to solve a take-apart word problem.

1 What number is the total? What part do you know? Complete the model at the right.

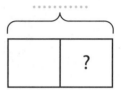

2 Complete the two equations for the model.

.... + ? = 15   15 − .... = ?

3 How many boys are on the team? Tell how you know.

4 Why can you add or subtract to solve the problem on the previous page?

5 REFLECT

Look back at your **Try It**, strategies by classmates, and **Picture It** and **Model It**. Which models or strategies do you like best for solving word problems? Explain.

....

....

....

APPLY IT
Use what you just learned to solve these problems.

6 Jen has 12 pencils. 7 are blue and the rest are white. How many white pencils does she have?

Write an equation to solve. Show your work.

Solution ....

7 Fiona has 13 books. What is one way she could give all the books to her brother and her sister? Show your work.

Solution ....

....

8 Kendra has 17 stickers. She gives some stickers to her friends. Then she has 9 stickers left. Which equations could you solve to find how many stickers Kendra has left?

Ⓐ $17 = ? - 9$

Ⓑ $? = 17 - 9$

Ⓒ $17 = 9 + ?$

Ⓓ $17 = ? + 9$

Ⓔ $? = 17 + 9$

Practice Solving Take-Apart Word Problems

Study the Example showing one way to solve a take-apart word problem. Then solve problems 1–5.

EXAMPLE

A cart has 14 books. There are 6 books on the bottom shelf. The rest are on the top shelf. How many books are on the top shelf?

You can use a bar model.

total
part	part

Write what you know.

14
6	?

Write an equation. Solve.

$14 - 6 = ?$

$14 - 6 = 8$

There are 8 books on the top shelf.

1 Complete the bar model for the Example problem. Then complete the equation.

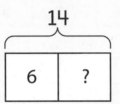

$14 = \underline{\hspace{1.5cm}} + \underline{\hspace{1.5cm}}$

2 Look at the equation you wrote in problem 1. Explain what your equation says about the books in the Example.

3 Rik picked 16 apples. He keeps 9 apples. He gives the rest to friends. How many apples does Rik give his friends?

Choose *Yes* or *No* to tell if each piece of information is given in the problem.

	Yes	No
the number of apples Rik picked	Ⓐ	Ⓑ
the number of apples Rik gives his friends	Ⓒ	Ⓓ
the number of apples Rik ate	Ⓔ	Ⓕ
the number of apples Rik keeps	Ⓖ	Ⓗ

4 Look at problem 3. Complete the bar model and solve the problem. Tell how you found your answer.

16

Rik gave his friends .... apples.

5 There are 11 frogs that live in 2 different tanks. How many frogs could be in each tank? Show your work.

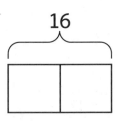

Solution ....

....

Develop Solving Comparison Word Problems

Read and try to solve the problem below.

> A small bag holds 3 fewer soccer balls than a big bag. The small bag holds 9 soccer balls. How many balls does the big bag hold?

TRY IT

 Math Toolkit
- counters
- ten frames
- blank bar models

DISCUSS IT

Ask your partner: Do you agree with me or not? Why or why not?

Tell your partner: I knew . . . so I . . .

Explore different ways to understand solving comparison word problems.

> **A small bag holds 3 fewer soccer balls than a big bag. The small bag holds 9 soccer balls. How many balls does the big bag hold?**

EXPLAIN IT
You can write what you know and do not know.

Know: small bag = **9** balls

Know: small bag + **3** = big bag

Find: How many balls are in the big bag?

PICTURE IT
You can draw a picture.

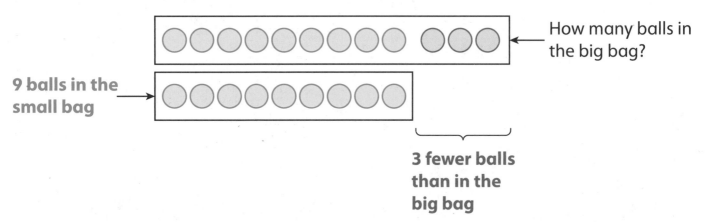

9 balls in the small bag

How many balls in the big bag?

3 fewer balls than in the big bag

CONNECT IT

Now you will use the problem from the previous page to help you understand how to write an equation to solve a comparison word problem.

1 How many balls does the small bag hold? ....

2 How many more balls does the big bag hold than the

small bag? ....

3 Write an addition equation to solve the problem. What does the equation show?

4 Can you write a subtraction equation to find the answer to this problem? Explain.

5 REFLECT

Look back at your **Try It**, strategies by classmates, and **Explain It** and **Picture It**. Which models or strategies do you like best for solving comparison word problems? Explain.

APPLY IT

Use what you just learned to solve these problems.

6 Ted has 8 white balloons and Mike has 6 red balloons. How many more balloons does Ted have than Mike? Show your work.

Solution ....

7 Explain how you would solve this problem.

Ken has 10 toy cars. He has 4 more toy cars than Sarah. How many toy cars does Sarah have?

8 Sally has some large pictures and 9 small pictures. She has 5 fewer large pictures than small pictures. How many large pictures does Sally have?

Ⓐ 4

Ⓑ 5

Ⓒ 9

Ⓓ 14

Practice Solving Comparison Word Problems

Study the Example showing a way to solve a comparison word problem. Then solve problems 1–4.

EXAMPLE

Maya has 4 hamsters and some mice. She has 3 fewer hamsters than mice. How many mice does Maya have?

Think about what you know.

There are **3 fewer hamsters** than mice.
That means there are **3 more mice** than hamsters.

Draw a picture.

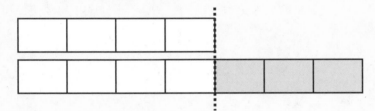

Write an equation. $4 + 3 = 7$

Maya has 7 mice.

1　There are 4 fewer markers than crayons. Circle *fewer* or *more* to complete each sentence.

There are 4 fewer/more markers than crayons.

That means there are 4 fewer/more crayons than markers.

2 There are 4 fewer markers than crayons. There are 6 markers. How many crayons are there? Show your work.

Solution ....

3 There are 8 children standing. There are 3 fewer children standing than sitting. How many children are sitting?

Ⓐ 3

Ⓑ 5

Ⓒ 8

Ⓓ 11

4 Dara has 12 counters. Diego has 7 counters. How many fewer counters does Diego have? Show your work.

Solution ....

Refine Solving Different Kinds of Word Problems

Complete the Example below. Then solve problems 1–3.

EXAMPLE

Sue scores 13 points. On her next turn, she loses 6 points. How many points does Sue have now?

You can draw a picture.

Sue's points ●●●●●●●●●//////

points scored − points lost = points Sue has now

13 − 6 = 7

Solution ....

APPLY IT

1 There are 14 dogs at the dog park. There are 6 black dogs. The rest are brown. How many brown dogs are at the dog park? Show your work.

Solution ....

2 Kim has 12 stickers. She gives some to her sister. Now Kim has 6 stickers left. How many stickers does Kim give her sister? Show your work.

> You can add or subtract to find the answer.

Solution ....

3 Kyle has some fish in a tank. Ana puts 4 more fish in the tank. Now there are 11 fish in the tank. How many fish were in the tank to begin with?

Ⓐ 4

Ⓑ 7

Ⓒ 8

Ⓓ 15

Deb chose Ⓑ as the correct answer. How did Deb get her answer?

> Were there fewer or more in the tank to begin with?

Practice Solving Different Kinds of Word Problems

1 Sid has 17 flowers. He sells some flowers. Now he has 9 flowers. How many flowers did he sell?

Choose *Yes* or *No* to tell if each piece of information is given in the problem.

It could be helpful to underline the information given in the problem.

	Yes	No
the number of flowers Sid started with	Ⓐ	Ⓑ
the number of flowers Sid sells	Ⓒ	Ⓓ
the number of flowers Sid has now	Ⓔ	Ⓕ

2 Sid has 17 flowers. He sells some flowers. Now he has 9 flowers. How many flowers did he sell?

You can count on or subtract to find the answer.

Ⓐ 6

Ⓑ 7

Ⓒ 8

Ⓓ 9

3 Juan has 9 quarters. How many quarters can he put in his red bank and how many quarters can he put in his blue bank? Show your work.

What do you know?

Solution ....

....

4 Lin has 4 pinecones and some acorns. She has 7 fewer pinecones than acorns. How many acorns does Lin have?

Does Lin have more pinecones or acorns?

Ⓐ 3

Ⓑ 4

Ⓒ 7

Ⓓ 11

Tom chose Ⓐ. How did Tom get his answer?

Refine Solving Different Kinds of Word Problems

APPLY IT
Solve the problems.

1 There are 4 children on a rug. More children join them. Now there are 10 children on the rug. How many children joined the first 4 children?

Ⓐ 4

Ⓑ 5

Ⓒ 6

Ⓓ 14

2 There are 5 cows in the barn. There are 8 more cows in the field than in the barn. How many cows are in the field?

Ⓐ 3   Ⓑ 8

Ⓒ 12   Ⓓ 13

3 Jin has 9 markers. He has 5 more markers than pencils. How many pencils does Jin have?

Choose *Yes* or *No* to tell if each equation could be used to solve the problem.

	Yes	No
$9 - 5 = 4$	Ⓐ	Ⓑ
$9 + 5 = 14$	Ⓒ	Ⓓ
$14 - 5 = 9$	Ⓔ	Ⓕ
$5 + 4 = 9$	Ⓖ	Ⓗ

4 Rick has some marbles in a bag. He adds 4 marbles to the bag. Now he has 13 marbles. How many marbles did Rick start with?

Fill in the blanks. Then choose all the equations that can be used to solve the problem.

Ⓐ $13 - 4 =$ ....

Ⓑ $13 -$ .... $= 4$

Ⓒ $13 + 4 =$ ....

Ⓓ .... $+ 4 = 13$

5 Write a problem that can be solved using the bar model at the right. Then show how to solve your problem.

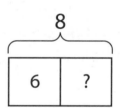

6 MATH JOURNAL

If the 8 in the bar model above changed to 9, how would this change your story? How would this change your answer?

☑ SELF CHECK Go back to the Unit 1 Opener and see what you can check off.

Draw and Use Bar Graphs and Picture Graphs

Dear Family,

This week your child is learning about picture graphs and bar graphs.

Picture graphs and bar graphs are two ways to show data, or collections of information.

The **picture graph** at the right shows there were 3 sunny days, 1 rainy day, 2 cloudy days, and 1 snowy day during a week. Each symbol represents 1 day.

Weather Last Week

Sunny	☀ ☀ ☀
Rainy	🌧
Cloudy	☁ ☁
Snowy	❄

The **bar graph** at the right shows the favorite fruits of 10 friends. The height of each bar tells how many friends prefer each type of fruit.

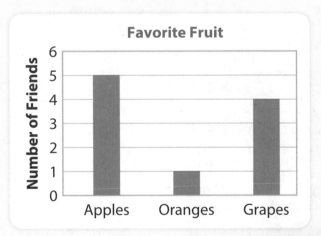

Invite your child to share what he or she knows about graphs by doing the following activity together.

 **ACTIVITY** **GRAPH**

Do the following activity with your child to draw bar graphs and picture graphs.

Materials 10–12 coins, markers

Practice making a picture graph and a bar graph with your child.

- Gather 10–12 different coins.

- Have your child sort the pennies, nickels, dimes, and quarters and count the number of each type of coin.

- Complete the picture graph and the bar graph below with the data. To complete the picture graph, draw circles with the letters *P*, *N*, *D*, and *Q* to show each coin.

- Ask your child questions about the data. For example, ask: *How many more pennies are there than nickels?*

Coins

Pennies	
Nickels	
Dimes	
Quarters	

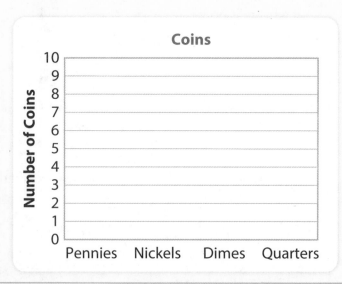

Coins

Number of Coins: 10, 9, 8, 7, 6, 5, 4, 3, 2, 1, 0 — Pennies, Nickels, Dimes, Quarters

Explore Drawing and Using Bar Graphs and Picture Graphs

You know how to add and subtract to solve problems. Use what you know to try to solve the problem below.

Parker asks his friends to tell him their favorite vegetable. He organizes their answers in a picture graph. How many friends choose carrots or beans?

Favorite Vegetables

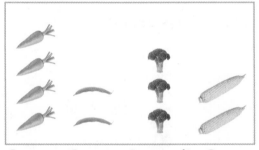

Carrots   Beans   Broccoli   Corn

TRY IT

 Math Toolkit
• counters
• connecting cubes

DISCUSS IT

Ask your partner: Do you agree with me? Why or why not?

Tell your partner: I agree with you about . . . because . . .

CONNECT IT

1 LOOK BACK

How did you find the number of friends who choose carrots or beans?

2 LOOK AHEAD

A **bar graph** uses bars to show data.

a. What do the labels under each bar show?

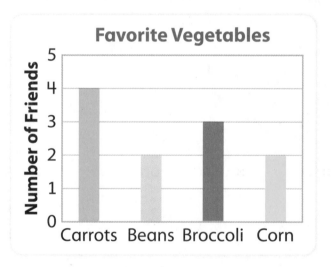

b. How many friends choose

broccoli? ....

3 REFLECT

How are the bar graph and the **picture graph** the same?

....

....

....

Prepare for Drawing and Using Graphs

1 Think about what you know about data. Fill in each box. Use words, numbers, and pictures. Show as many ideas as you can.

Word	In My Own Words	Example
data		
bar graph		
picture graph		

2 Do the bar graph and the picture graph show the same data? Explain.

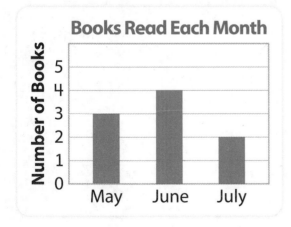

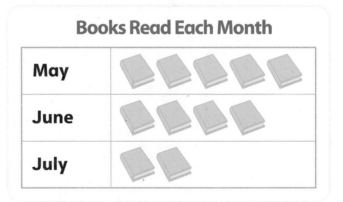

3 Solve the problem. Show your work.

Hana asks her friends to tell her their favorite fruit. She organizes their answers in a picture graph. How many friends choose apples or bananas?

Favorite Fruits

Apples	🍎 🍎 🍎
Grapes	🍇
Bananas	🍌 🍌
Oranges	🍊 🍊 🍊

Solution ....

4 Check your answer. Show your work.

Develop Using Bar Graphs and Picture Graphs

Read and try to solve the problem below.

Martin asks the students in his class: *What is your favorite sport?* **He makes a picture graph and a bar graph to show his results. How many students does Martin ask?**

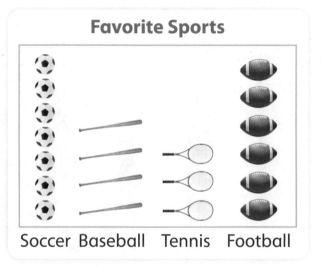

Favorite Sports

Soccer Baseball Tennis Football

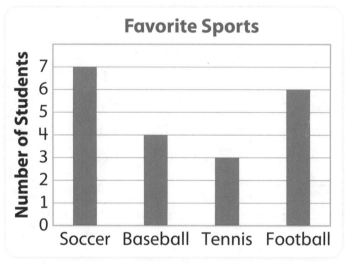

Favorite Sports

Number of Students

7
6
5
4
3
2
1
0

Soccer Baseball Tennis Football

TRY IT

 Math Toolkit
- counters
- 10-frames
- connecting cubes

DISCUSS IT

Ask your partner: How did you get started?

Tell your partner: At first, I thought . . .

Explore different ways to understand using bar graphs and picture graphs.

> **Martin asks the students in his class:** *What is your favorite sport?* **He makes a picture graph and a bar graph to show his results. How many students does Martin ask?**

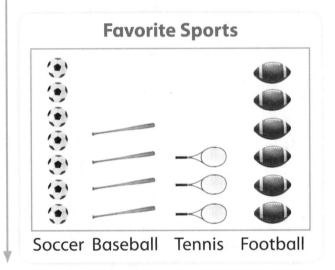

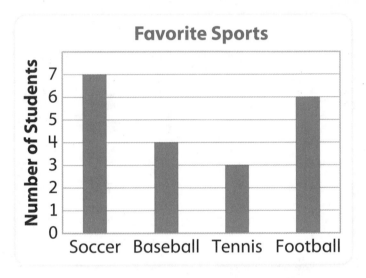

PICTURE IT

You can add the totals of the pictures in the picture graph.

You can add the totals of each bar in the bar graph.

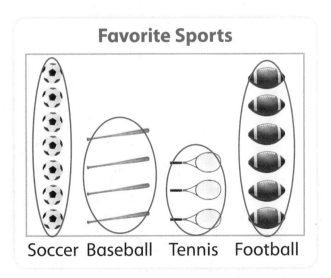

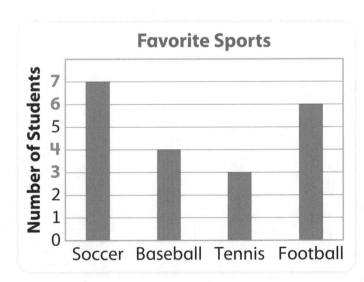

CONNECT IT

Now you will use the problem from the previous page to help you understand more about bar graphs and picture graphs.

1 How do you use the picture graph to find the number of students who choose soccer?

2 How do you use the bar graph to find the number of students who choose soccer?

3 How many students choose soccer as their

favorite sport? ....

4 How many students does Martin ask? Explain how to use the bar graph to find your answer.

5 REFLECT

Look back at your **Try It**, strategies by classmates, and **Picture It**. Which type of graph do you like best for solving a problem about data? Explain.

....

....

APPLY IT

Use what you just learned to solve these problems.

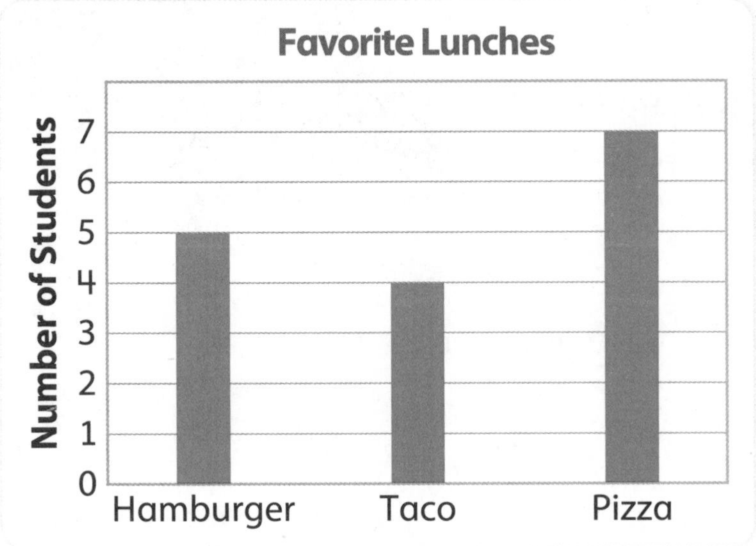
Favorite Lunches
Number of Students
0
1
2
3
4
5
6
7
Hamburger
Taco
Pizza

6 How many fewer students choose taco than pizza? ....

7 How many students choose hamburger or pizza? ....

8 Which statements are true about the data in the graph?

Ⓐ 3 more students choose pizza than taco.

Ⓑ Hamburger gets the most votes.

Ⓒ 1 fewer student chooses taco than hamburger.

Ⓓ 12 students choose hamburger or taco.

Ⓔ 17 students vote in all.

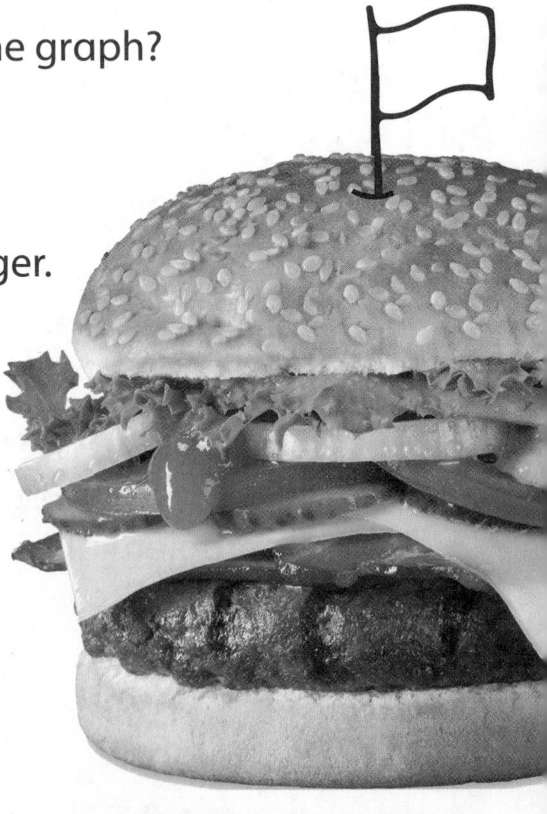

Practice Using Bar Graphs and Picture Graphs

Study the Example showing how to use a bar graph. Then solve problems 1–13.

EXAMPLE

Val counts the shapes of her stickers. She makes a bar graph. How many of her stickers are circles?

The bar for circles goes up to the line for 6.

Val has 6 circle stickers.

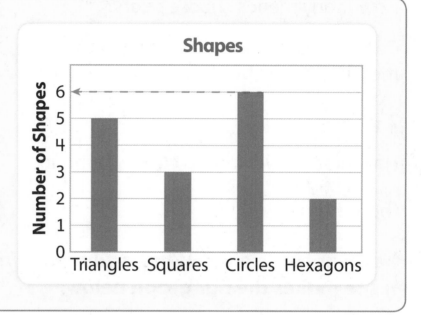

Use the information from the Example to answer problems 1–4.

1. How many triangles does Val have? ....

2. How many hexagons does Val have? ....

3. Complete the equation to show how many more triangles than hexagons Val has.

   5 − .... = ...

4. Write an equation to show how many squares and circles Val has in all.

   .... + ... = ...

> **Vocabulary**
>
> **bar graph** a data display in which bars are used to show the number of items in each category.

**Saul asks his friends: *What is your favorite fruit?*
Then he makes the picture graph below.**

5 How many friends choose apples? ....

6 How many friends choose pears? ....

7 Complete the equation to show how many
friends choose apples or pears.

   7 + ... = ...

8 How many fewer friends choose bananas

   than cherries? ....

Favorite Fruits

Apple   Banana   Pear   Cherry

**Rachel asks her friends: *What is your favorite instrument?*
Then she makes the bar graph below.**

9 How many friends choose piano?

   ....

10 How many friends choose drums?

   ....

11 How many more friends choose

   piano than drums? ....

12 How many fewer friends choose

   trumpet than guitar? ....

13 How many friends does Rachel ask? ....

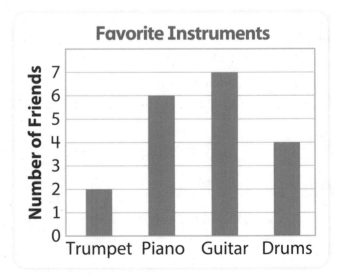

Favorite Instruments

Number of Friends

Trumpet   Piano   Guitar   Drums

Develop Making Bar Graphs and Picture Graphs

Read and try to solve the problem below.

> **Lynn visits an apple orchard. She looks at one row of trees. She writes down the color of the apples on each tree. Show one way that Lynn could organize the data. Then make a graph to show the data.**
>
> red, red, yellow, green, red, green,
> red, red, yellow, red, green, green

TRY IT

 Math Toolkit
• connecting cubes
• grid paper

DISCUSS IT

Ask your partner: Why did you choose that strategy?

Tell your partner: A model I used was ... It helped me ...

Explore different ways to understand making bar graphs and picture graphs.

> **Lynn visits an apple orchard. She looks at one row of trees. She writes down the color of the apples on each tree. Show one way that Lynn could organize the data. Then make a graph to show the data.**
>
> red, red, yellow, green, red, green,
> red, red, yellow, red, green, green

MODEL IT

You can organize the data in a tally chart.

Red	Yellow	Green
⊥⊥⊥ I	II	IIII

MODEL IT

You can organize the data in a table.

Color of Apple	Number of Trees
Red	6
Yellow	2
Green	4

CONNECT IT

Now you will use the problem from the previous page to make bar graphs and picture graphs.

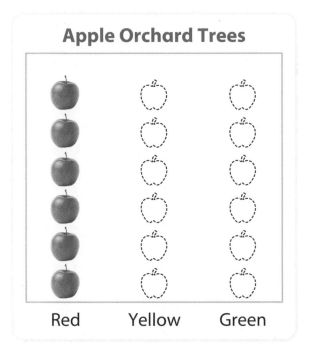

Apple Orchard Trees

Red   Yellow   Green

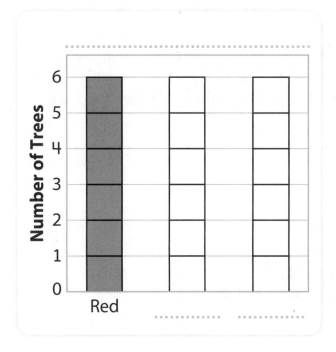

Number of Trees

6
5
4
3
2
1
0

Red

1 Complete the picture graph by coloring the apples.

2 On the bar graph, fill in the title and labels.

3 Complete the bar graph by coloring the bars.

4 REFLECT

Look back at your **Try It**, strategies by classmates, **Model Its**, and **Connect It**. Which models or strategies do you like best for organizing data and showing data in a graph?

APPLY IT

Use what you just learned to solve these problems.

5 Make a bar graph for the favorite color data.

Favorite Colors			
Blue	**Purple**	**Green**	**Red**
5	6	3	2

6 Make a picture graph to show the favorite color data.

7 One student changes his favorite color from blue to green. How will this change your bar graph? How will this change your picture graph? Explain.

Practice Making Bar Graphs and Picture Graphs

Study the Example showing how to make a bar graph from a tally chart. Then solve problems 1–8.

EXAMPLE

Mia makes the tally chart below to show the colors of heart stickers she has. Then she makes the bar graph.

Yellow	Pink	Red
III	II	IIII

Mia writes the title of her graph above it.

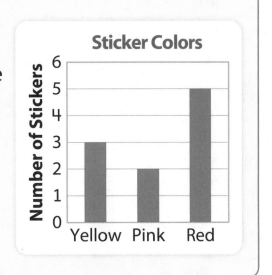

Mia wants to make a picture graph. Use the data in Mia's tally chart.

1. Write a title on the line above the graph.

2. Write the missing color name next to *Yellow* and *Pink*.

3. Draw the correct number of hearts above the word *Yellow*.

4. Draw the correct number of hearts above the word *Pink*.

Carter makes this tally chart to show the colors of flowers in his window box. Use the data in Carter's tally chart to complete the bar graph.

White	Purple	Orange
IIII	IHHI	III

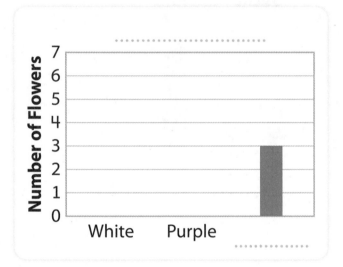

5 What is a good title for the graph? Write it on the line above the graph.

6 Write the missing color name next to *White* and *Purple*.

7 Draw a bar to show how many white flowers there are.

8 Draw a bar to show how many purple flowers there are.

Vocabulary

data a set of collected information.

Refine Drawing and Using Graphs

Complete the Example below. Then solve problems 1–3.

EXAMPLE

Gavin makes a picture graph to show the stickers he has. How many more stars does Gavin have than dots?

Stickers

Moon	🌙
Heart	❤ ❤ ❤ ❤ ❤
Star	⭐ ⭐ ⭐ ⭐ ⭐ ⭐ ⭐ ⭐
Dot	● ●

Look at how you can show your work.

$8 - 2 = 6$

Solution ....

APPLY IT

1 How many stickers does Gavin have that are stars or hearts? Show your work.

> How many star stickers are there? How many heart stickers? Find the total.

Solution ....

Lesson 4 Draw and Use Bar Graphs and Picture Graphs

2 Ally makes this graph on Sunday morning. Then she reads 2 more books that day. Fill in the graph to show that she reads 2 more books on Sunday.

What is the total number of books for Sunday?

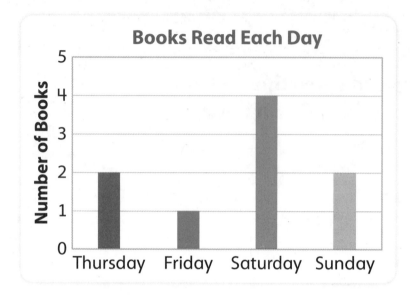

3 How many fewer books did Ally read on Friday than on Saturday?

What data do you need to look at?

Ⓐ 1

Ⓑ 2

Ⓒ 3

Ⓓ 4

John chose Ⓐ as the correct answer. How did John get his answer?

Practice Drawing and Using Graphs

1 Tia makes this picture graph to show the bead shapes in her collection. Then her mom gives her 3 more flower beads. Fill in the graph to show how many flower beads Tia has now.

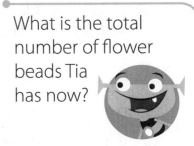

What is the total number of flower beads Tia has now?

Bead Shapes

Hearts	♥ ♥ ♥ ♥ ♥ ♥ ♥
Flowers	✹
Moons	☾ ☾
Stars	★

2 Use the picture graph from problem 1 to answer the questions below.

How many more hearts does Tia have than moons?

Ⓐ 7

Ⓑ 5

Ⓒ 3

Ⓓ 2

What are the numbers you will use to find the solution?

Fiona chose Ⓐ. How did Fiona get her answer?

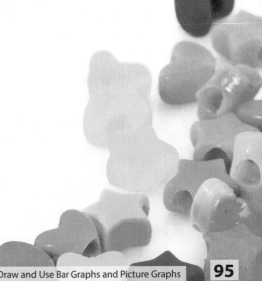

3 Milo records the number of journal pages he writes each day in the tally chart below.

Sunday	Monday	Tuesday
卌 I	III	IIII

Use the tally chart to complete the bar graph.

- Draw the two missing bars.
- Write the missing day.
- Give the graph a title.

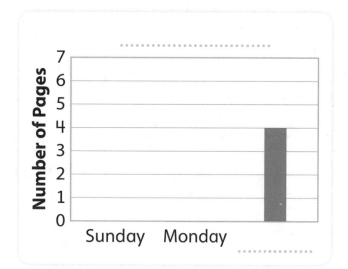

> What can you look at on the bar graph to help you draw each bar the correct height?

4 Look at the data in problem 3.

How many fewer pages does Milo write on Tuesday than on Sunday?

.... pages

> Can you use an equation to find how many fewer pages Milo writes?

Refine Drawing and Using Bar Graphs and Picture Graphs

APPLY IT

Solve the problems.

Maggie records the hair color of the girls on her softball team. She puts her data in a bar graph at the right.

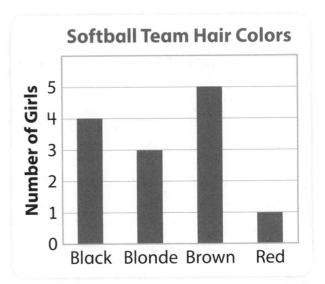

Softball Team Hair Colors

1. Which two colors have the least number of girls with that hair color?

   Ⓐ black and blonde

   Ⓑ brown and black

   Ⓒ black and red

   Ⓓ red and blonde

2. Choose *True* or *False* for each sentence.

	True	False
There are more girls with black hair than brown hair.	Ⓐ	Ⓑ
There are 15 girls on Maggie's soccer team.	Ⓒ	Ⓓ
There are 2 fewer girls with red hair than blonde hair.	Ⓔ	Ⓕ
There are 8 girls with brown hair or blonde hair.	Ⓖ	Ⓗ

3 Wes records the weather for one week in the table at the right.

Complete the picture graph below using the data in the table. Draw a ☼ for sunny days and a ☁ for cloudy days.

Sunny, Cloudy, and Rainy Days	
Sunny	
....	
Rainy	💧 💧

Day	Weather
Sun.	cloudy
Mon.	cloudy
Tue.	sunny
Wed.	rainy
Thu.	rainy
Fri.	sunny
Sat.	cloudy

4 If Saturday had been sunny, how would the picture graph be different than it is now?

5 MATH JOURNAL

Write an addition problem using the data about the weather. Then explain how to solve your problem.

☑ SELF CHECK Go back to the Unit 1 Opener and see what you can check off.

Solve Two-Step Word Problems

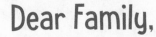

Dear Family,

This week your child is learning to solve two-step word problems using models along with addition and subtraction equations.

Consider this word problem: *There are 17 flowers in a vase. 8 flowers are daisies. 3 are roses. The rest are mums. How many are mums?*

There are multiple ways to solve this two-step problem.

- You could solve by first subtracting the number of daisies from the total number of flowers.

    17 − 8 = 9

    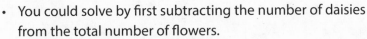

    Then you subtract the number of roses.

    9 − 3 = 6

    There are 6 mums.

- You also could solve the problem by adding the number of daisies and roses first and then subtracting that number from the total number of flowers.

    8 + 3 = 11   **17 − 11 = 6**

    There are 6 mums.

    Invite your child to share what he or she knows about solving two-step word problems by doing the following activity together.

ACTIVITY SOLVING TWO-STEP WORD PROBLEMS

Do this activity with your child to solve two-step word problems.

Materials paper and pencil, ingredients for a punch or snack mix (optional)

With your child, pretend you are making a snack mix and fruit punch for a party using the ingredients below. Ask your child to help you solve each word problem.

1. You want to make 10 cups of snack mix. You have 4 cups of walnuts and 4 cups of raisins. How many cups of chocolate chips do you need?

2. You need 6 cups of fruit punch. Use 2 cups of pineapple juice. Add 1 cup of cranberry juice. How many cups of orange juice should you add?

Answers: **1.** 2 cups; **2.** 3 cups

Explore Solving Two-Step Word Problems

You have solved one-step word problems in equations. Use what you know to try to solve the problem below.

> **Eve has 3 striped banners and 3 dotted banners. Then she makes 7 white banners. How many banners does Eve have now?**

TRY IT

 Math Toolkit
- connecting cubes
- counters
- 10-frames
- number bonds
- number lines

DISCUSS IT

Ask your partner: Can you explain that again?

Tell your partner: I am not sure how to find the answer because . . .

CONNECT IT

1 LOOK BACK

How many banners does Eve have now? ....

2 LOOK AHEAD

You need two steps to solve some problems. Here is another example.

Juan has 3 pink markers and 7 green markers. He loses 2 markers. How many markers does he have now?

a. Why would you start this problem with $3 + 7 = 10$?

b. What is the next step? Complete the subtraction equation.

$$10 - \underline{\quad\quad} = \underline{\quad\quad}$$

c. How many markers does Juan have now? ....

3 Why is this problem a two-step problem?

4 REFLECT

Look at the two equations in problems 2a and 2b. Why is 10 in both equations?

....

....

Prepare for Solving Two-Step Word Problems

1 Think about what you know about solving word problems.
Fill in each box. Use words, numbers, and pictures. Show as
many ideas as you can.

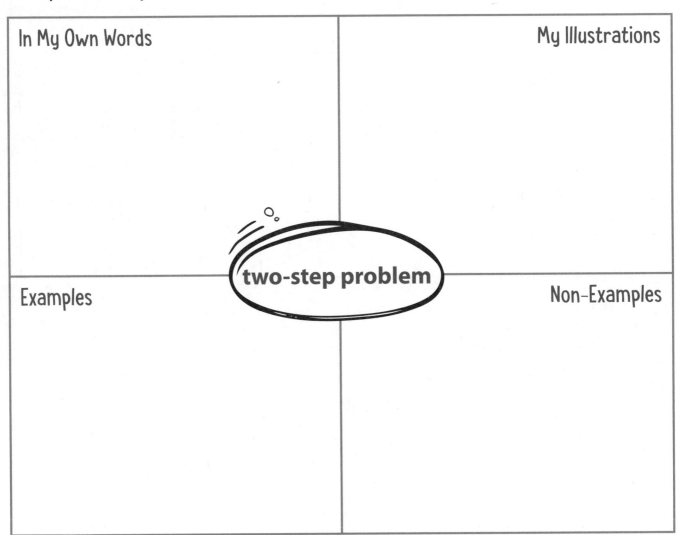

In My Own Words	My Illustrations
Examples	Non-Examples

two-step problem

2 Julia has 3 red marbles and 8 blue marbles. Then she
loses 2 marbles. How many marbles does she have now?

What are the two steps to solve this problem?

3 Solve the problem. Show your work.

Benny has 2 blue balloons and 5 yellow balloons. Then he buys 8 green balloons. How many balloons does Benny have now?

Solution ....

4 Check your answer. Show your work.

Develop Ways to Solve Two-Step Problems

Read and try to solve the problem below.

> Meg has 8 pears in her basket. Then she picks
> 6 more pears. After that, she gives away 5 pears
> to her friends. How many pears are in the
> basket now?

TRY IT

 Math Toolkit
- connecting cubes
- counters
- 10-frames
- number bonds
- number lines

DISCUSS IT

Ask your partner:
Do you agree with
me? Why or why
not?

Tell your partner:
I disagree with this
part because . . .

Explore different ways to understand solving two-step word problems.

> **Meg has 8 pears in her basket. Then she picks 6 more pears. After that, she gives away 5 pears to her friends. How many pears are in the basket now?**

PICTURE IT
You can draw a picture.

Step 1:   8 pears + 6 more pears

Step 2:   14 pears − 5 pears given away

MODEL IT
You can make a bar model.

Step 1:

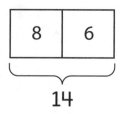

Step 2:

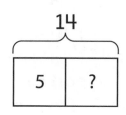

CONNECT IT

Now you will use the problem from the previous page to help you understand how to solve two-step problems using equations.

1 Look at **Picture It**. Write an equation for Step 1.

.... + ... = ...

2 Look at **Model It**. Write an equation for Step 2.

.... − .... = ?

3 How many pears are in the basket now? ....

4 How is a two-step problem different from a one-step problem?

5 REFLECT

Look back at your **Try It**, strategies by classmates, and **Picture It** and **Model It**. Which models or strategies do you like best for solving two-step problems? Explain.

....

....

....

....

APPLY IT

Use what you just learned to solve these problems.

6 There are 12 boys in the pool. Then 3 go home. Then 6 more boys jump in the pool. How many boys are in the pool now? Show your work.

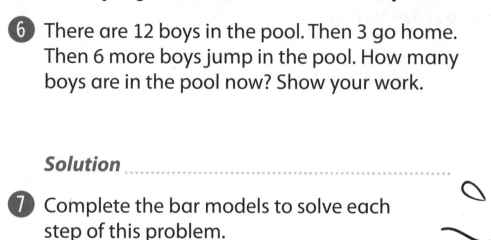

Solution ....

7 Complete the bar models to solve each step of this problem.

Millie has $15. She spends $6 for lunch. Then she spends $4 for a train ticket. How much money does Millie have left? Show your work.

Step 1:

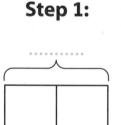

Step 2:

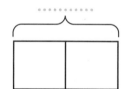

Millie has $............ left.

8 Andy reads 5 books in June and 7 books in July. Then he reads 4 more books in August. How many books does Andy read in all three months?

  Ⓐ 8   Ⓑ 11

  Ⓒ 12   Ⓓ 16

Practice Ways to Solve Two-Step Problems

Study the Example showing one way to solve a two-step problem. Then solve problems 1–4.

EXAMPLE

There are 7 balls in the gym closet. Then 3 balls are taken out. After class, 9 balls are returned. How many balls are in the closet now?

Step 1:

7 balls − 3 balls = **4 balls**

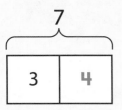

Step 2:

4 balls + 9 balls = 13 balls

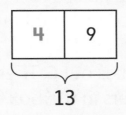

So, there are 13 balls in the closet now.

Jay has 13 posters to hang. He hangs 5 in the morning. Then he hangs 4 more in the afternoon. How many posters does Jay have left to hang?

1 Circle an equation for Step 1.

Underline an equation for Step 2.

$5 - 4 = 1$ $13 + 5 = 18$

$8 - 4 = 4$ $13 - 5 = 8$

2 Jay has .... posters left.

3 There are 15 people on a train. At the first stop, 8 people get off the train and 3 people get on. How many people are on the train now?

Complete the bar models. Show your work.

15

Step 1:

Step 2:

Solution

4 A box holds 12 markers. Nan takes out 6. Then she puts 2 back. Are there enough markers in the box for Fen to take out 10? Show your work.

Solution

Develop More Ways to Solve Two-Step Problems

Read and try to solve the problem below.

> There are 16 quarters in a jar. Russ takes
> 6 quarters. Then Dad adds more quarters to
> the jar. Now, there are 18 quarters in the jar.
> How many does Dad put in?

TRY IT

 **Math Toolkit**
- connecting cubes
- counters
- 10-frames
- bar models
- number lines

DISCUSS IT

Ask your partner:
How did you get
started?

Tell your partner:
At first, I thought . . .

Explore more ways to understand solving two-step word problems.

> **There are 16 quarters in a jar. Russ takes 6 quarters. Then Dad adds more quarters to the jar. Now, there are 18 quarters in the jar. How many does Dad put in?**

PICTURE IT

You can draw a picture.

Step 1:   There are 16 quarters in a jar.
Russ takes 6 quarters.

Step 2:   Then Dad adds more quarters to the jar.
Now, there are 18 quarters in the jar.

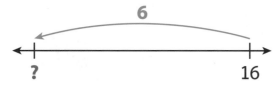

MODEL IT

You can use open number lines.

Step 1:   There are 16 quarters in a jar.
Russ takes 6 quarters.

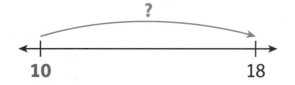

6

?   16

Step 2:   Then Dad adds more quarters to the jar.
Now, there are 18 quarters in the jar.

?

10   18

CONNECT IT

Now you will use the problem from the previous page to help you understand more ways to solve two-step word problems.

1 Look at the number line in Step 1 of **Model It**.

Complete the equation. $16 - 6 =$ ....

2 Write an equation for Step 2.

.... $+ ? =$ ....

3 How many quarters did Dad put in the jar? ....

4 Explain how to solve a two-step problem.

5 REFLECT

Look back at your **Try It**, strategies by classmates, and **Picture It** and **Model It**. Which models or strategies do you like best for solving two-step problems? Explain.

....

....

....

APPLY IT

Use what you just learned to solve these problems.

6 Javier has 7 shells. Then he finds 4 more. Then some shells break. Now Javier has 9 shells. How many shells break? Show your work.

Solution ....

7 Complete the number lines to solve each step of this problem.

Diane puts 4 daisies and 5 roses in a vase. Then she adds some carnations. Now, there are 17 flowers in the vase. How many carnations does Diane put in the vase?

Step 1:   **Step 2:**

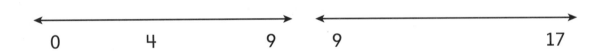

0   4   9   9   17

Diane put .... carnations in the vase.

8 Which equations could you use in solving this problem?

Karl buys 5 tickets to a show. Then he buys 10 more tickets. He gives some tickets to his friends. Now Karl has 9 tickets. How many tickets does Karl give to his friends?

Ⓐ $10 + 5 = 15$ Ⓑ $10 - 5 = 5$

Ⓒ $15 - 9 = 6$ Ⓓ $6 + 10 = 16$

Ⓔ $10 - 9 = 1$

Practice More Ways to Solve Two-Step Problems

Study the Example showing one way to solve two-step problems. Then solve problems 1–5.

EXAMPLE

There are 8 bananas on the counter. Someone takes 3 bananas. Another person puts 4 bananas on the counter. How many bananas are there now?

Step 1:   8 bananas − 3 bananas

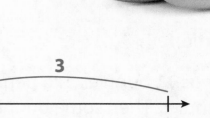

Step 2:   There are 5 bananas.
There are 4 more bananas.

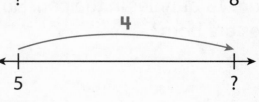

There are 9 bananas on the counter now.

1 Look at the Example. Then complete the equations to show Step 1 and Step 2.

Step 1   8 − .... = ...

Step 2   .... + 4 = ...

2 Think about the Example. Could you do Step 2 first? Explain.

3 There are 9 players on the field. Then 6 more players come to the field. They make two teams. There are 8 players on one team. How many are on the other team? Show your work.

Solution ....

4 Val has 11 bunnies in a pen. Then he sells 4 bunnies. Then some bunnies are born. Now there are 13 bunnies in the pen. How many bunnies are born?

Ⓐ 6

Ⓑ 7

Ⓒ 8

Ⓓ 9

5 Look at problem 4. If Val has 14 bunnies at the end instead of 13 bunnies, would Step 1 change? Would Step 2 change? Explain.

Refine Solving Two-Step Word Problems

Complete the Example below. Then solve problems 1–3.

EXAMPLE

Emma has 12 cards and Stan has 0. Emma gives Stan some of her cards. Now Emma has 9 cards. How many more cards does Emma have than Stan?

Look at how you can show your work.

Emma starts with 12 cards and
ends up with 9.

$12 - ? = 9$

$12 - 3 = 9$

So, Stan has 3 cards.

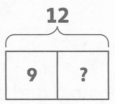

12

| 9 | ? |

Emma has 9 cards. Stan has
3 cards.

$9 - 3 = ?$

$9 - 3 = 6$

9

| 3 | ? |

Solution ....

APPLY IT

1 There are 6 toys in a box. Fritz takes 2 toys out of the box. Then he puts 8 toys into the box. How many toys are in the box now? Show your work.

Try acting out the problem.

Solution ....

2 Rob has 16 crayons. He gives 8 crayons to Troy. Ella gives Rob some crayons. Now Rob has 17 crayons. How many crayons does Ella give to Rob? Show your work.

How many crayons does Rob have after he gives some away? How many does he have now?

Solution

3 Bev gets 6 dollars from her mom and 4 dollars from her dad. She wants to buy a game that costs 18 dollars. How many more dollars does Bev need?

Ⓐ 2

Ⓑ 8

Ⓒ 10

Ⓓ 14

How can you find how much money Bev has?

Allie chose Ⓒ as the correct answer. How did Allie get her answer?

Practice Solving Two-Step Word Problems

1. There are 19 ducks in the pond. First, 9 ducks fly away. Then 3 more ducks fly away. How many ducks are in the pond now?

   Ⓐ 6

   Ⓑ 7

   Ⓒ 10

   Ⓓ 16

   > What do the ducks do in Step 1? In Step 2?

2. Will has 9 stickers. He gives 2 to Hasina. Then he puts some on his lunch bag. He has 4 stickers left. How many does Will put on his lunch bag?

   Ⓐ 3

   Ⓑ 5

   Ⓒ 7

   Ⓓ 11

   > Does Will have more or fewer stickers after he gives 2 to Hasina?

   Sam chose Ⓓ as the correct answer. How did Sam get her answer?

3 Sal has 8 balloons. He has 3 red balloons. The rest are blue. Kay has 5 more blue balloons than Sal. How many blue balloons does Kay have?

Ⓐ 6

Ⓑ 8

Ⓒ 10

Ⓓ 16

What do you need to find in Step 1?

4 Choose an equation.

$$3 + 8 = 11$$
$$15 - 6 = 9$$
$$2 + 5 = 7$$
$$9 - 4 = 5$$

Write a two-step word problem. Your equation must be used to solve one of the steps.

What are some actions that you would use plus or minus for?

Refine Solving Two-Step Word Problems

APPLY IT

Solve the problems.

1 Cara picks 11 big apples and 7 small apples. Dan picks 5 fewer apples than Cara. How many apples does Dan pick?

   Ⓐ 18   Ⓑ 6

   Ⓒ 13   Ⓓ 2

2 There are 15 birds on a branch. Then 6 birds fly away. Then 3 birds land on the branch. How many birds are on the branch now?

Fill in the blanks. Then circle all the answers that show a step in solving the problem.

   Ⓐ $15 + 6 =$ ....

   Ⓑ $15 - 6 =$ ....

   Ⓒ $9 - 3 =$ ....

   Ⓓ $9 + 3 =$ ....

3 Ana has 10 beads. She buys 3 more beads. Then Ana gives 7 beads to Beth. How many beads does Ana have now?

   Ⓐ 20   Ⓑ 13

   Ⓒ 6   Ⓓ 0

4 Lee has 8 square blocks and 9 triangle blocks. Jon takes some of Lee's blocks. Then Lee has 10 blocks left. How many blocks does Jon take?

Ⓐ 2

Ⓑ 7

Ⓒ 17

Ⓓ 27

5 A star card is worth 10 points. A moon card is worth 4 fewer points. How many points are a star card and moon card worth together? Show your work.

Solution ....

6 MATH JOURNAL

Write a two-step problem that uses addition and subtraction. Then explain how to solve your problem.

 SELF CHECK Go back to the Unit 1 Opener and see what you can check off.

In this unit you learned to . . .

Skill	Lesson
Count on to add and subtract.	1, 2
Use fact families to add and subtract.	2, 3, 5, 6
Make a ten to add and subtract.	2, 5
Solve a one-step word problem.	3
Draw and find information from pictures and bar graphs.	4
Use addition and subtraction to solve a problem with more than one step.	5

Think about what you learned.

Use words, numbers, and drawings.

1 Two important things I learned are . . .

2 Something I know well is . . .

3 I could use more practice with . . .

Solve Addition and Subtraction Problems

Study an Example Problem and Solution

SMP 1 Make sense of problems and persevere in solving them.

Read this problem about adding to or subtracting from to solve real-world problems. Then look at Plory's solution to the problem.

Robot Motors

Beau wants to build a shelf to store his 16 robot motors. Look at his plan.

Shelf Plan

- Use up to 6 shelves.
- Put at least 3 and no more than 6 robot motors on each shelf.

How many shelves should Beau make? How many motors should he put on each shelf?

Show how Plory's solution matches the checklist.

☑ PROBLEM-SOLVING CHECKLIST

- ☐ Tell what is known.
- ☐ Tell what the problem is asking.
- ☐ Show all your work.
- ☐ Show that the solution works.

a. **Circle** something that is known.

b. **Underline** something that you need to find.

c. **Draw a box around** what you do to solve the problem.

d. **Put a checkmark** next to the part that shows the solution works.

PLORY'S SOLUTION

Hi, I'm Plory. Here's how I solved the problem.

- **I know** I have 16 robot motors to put on up to 6 shelves. Each shelf holds from 3 to 6 motors.

- **I need to find** how many shelves to use and how many motors to put on each shelf.

- **I want to use** many shelves so there is room for more robot motors.

- **I can try** the fewest number of motors to put on a shelf, which is 3. I will start at 16 and keep subtracting 3 to find how many shelves I need.

$$16 - 3 = 13$$
$$13 - 3 = 10$$
$$10 - 3 = 7$$
$$7 - 3 = 4$$

$\left.\begin{array}{c} \\ \\ \\ \\ \end{array}\right\}$ 4 shelves

Each difference tells me how many motors are left to put on shelves.

There are 4 shelves with 3 motors on each shelf. That leaves 4 more motors.
I can add one more shelf with 4 motors.

- **Add** the motors on each shelf to check.

$$3 + 3 + 3 = 9$$
$$9 + 3 + 4 = 16$$

I subtracted to solve the problem. So I'll add to check the answer.

- **Use 4 shelves with 3 motors on each and 1 shelf with 4 motors.**

Try Another Approach

There are many ways to solve problems. Think about how you might solve the Robot Motors problem in a different way.

Robot Motors

Beau wants to build a shelf to store his 16 robot motors. Look at his plan.

Shelf Plan

- Use up to 6 shelves.
- Put at least 3 and no more than 6 robot motors on each shelf.

How many shelves should Beau make? How many motors should he put on each shelf?

PLAN IT

Answer this question to help you start thinking about a plan.

What numbers can you use for the number of shelves? Explain how you know.

SOLVE IT

Find a different solution for the Robot Motors problem.
Show all your work on a separate sheet of paper.

You may want to use the Problem-Solving Tips to get started.

PROBLEM-SOLVING TIPS

- **Questions**

  - Would I rather have fewer shelves or more shelves?

  - Do I want to put different numbers of motors on the shelves?

- **Word Bank**

fewest	add	total
most	subtract	difference

- **Sentence Starters**

  - I can use _____

  - I can put up to _____

☑ PROBLEM-SOLVING CHECKLIST

Make sure that you . . .

☐ tell what you know.

☐ tell what you need to do.

☐ show all your work.

☐ show that the solution works.

REFLECT

Use Mathematical Practices Talk about this question with a partner.

- **Use a Model** What addition or subtraction equations can you use to check your answer? What do they show?

Discuss Models and Strategies

**Solve the problem on a separate sheet of paper.
There are different ways you can solve it.**

Rock Collection

Beau made these graphs about his rock collection.
He wants to compare the different kinds of rocks in
his collection.

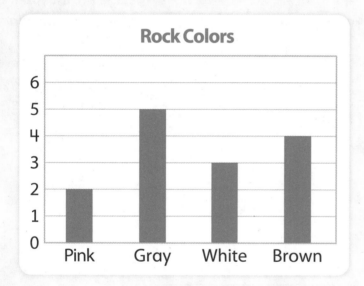

Rock Colors

Rock Shapes

Wide	⬠ ⬠ ⬠ ⬠ ⬠
Narrow	⬡ ⬡ ⬡ ⬡
Rounded	◯ ◯ ◯ ◯ ◯

What are some statements that Beau could write to
describe the numbers and kinds of rocks in his collection?

PLAN IT AND SOLVE IT

Find a solution to the Rock Collection problem.

- Write two or three statements that tell about the colors and shapes of the rocks.
- Show how you used the numbers in the graphs to write the statements.

You may want to use the Problem-Solving Tips to get started.

→ PROBLEM-SOLVING TIPS ←

- **Questions**

  - What do the numbers in the graph tell about the rocks?

  - How can I add and subtract numbers in the graph to help write statements?

- **Word Bank**

more	most	total
fewer	least	difference

- **Sentence Starters**

  - There are _____ more _____

  - There are fewer _____

✓ **PROBLEM-SOLVING CHECKLIST**

Make sure that you . . .
- ☐ tell what you know.
- ☐ tell what you need to do.
- ☐ show all your work.
- ☐ show that the solution works.

REFLECT

Use Mathematical Practices Talk about this question with a partner.

- **Think and Reason** How can you write equations to show that your statements are true?

Persevere On Your Own

Solve each problem on a separate sheet of paper.

Nuts and Bolts

Beau has 18 bolts. He has 3 boxes to put them in.
He wants to put at least 3 bolts in each box.

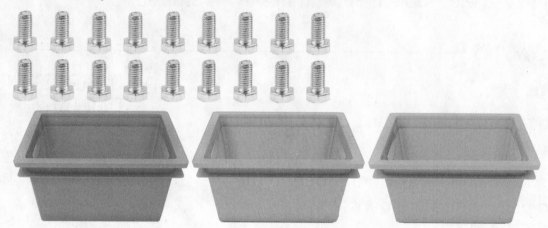

How many bolts can Beau put in each box?

SOLVE IT

Show one way that Beau can put the bolts in the boxes.

• Draw a picture.

• Tell how many bolts to put in each box.

• Explain why your answer works.

REFLECT

Use Mathematical Practices Talk about this question
with a partner.

• **Make Sense of Problems** How did you decide how
  many bolts to put in each box?

Science Project

Beau has 17 jars. He needs at least 8, but no more than 12 jars for a science project. He will put the rest of the jars on a shelf.

How many jars could Beau use for the science project?

How many will be left to put on the shelf?

SOLVE IT

Tell how many jars Beau could use and how many will be left to put on the shelf.

• Draw a picture.

• Circle a number of jars Beau that can use.

• Find the number of jars Beau will put on the shelf.

• Show that the total number of jars is 17.

REFLECT

Use Mathematical Practices Talk about this question with a partner.

• **Check Your Answer** What did you do to check that your answer makes sense?

1 Juan counts his paper shapes.

- He has 7 hearts.

- He has 3 fewer stars than hearts.

- He has 16 paper shapes in all.

Complete the picture graph to show Juan's paper shapes.

Juan's Paper Shapes	
Hearts	♡ ♡ ♡ ♡ ♡ ♡ ♡
Stars	
Dots	

2 Rosa has 17 flowers. She puts some flowers in a vase. Now Rosa has 9 flowers left. How many flowers did Rosa put in the vase?

Ⓐ 6

Ⓑ 8

Ⓒ 9

Ⓓ 26

3 Which expressions can be used to find $8 + 6$?
Choose all the correct answers.

Ⓐ $6 + 6 + 1$

Ⓑ $8 + 2 + 6$

Ⓒ $6 + 4 + 4$

Ⓓ $8 + 2 + 4$

Ⓔ $10 + 4$

4 There are 17 people on the bus. At the first stop,
9 people get off the bus and 4 people get on.
How many people are on the bus now?
Show your work.

5 Hector has a 15-visit pass to a museum. He visits
11 times. How many visits are left? Decide if each
equation could be used to solve this problem.
Choose *Yes* or *No* for each equation.

	Yes	No
$15 - ? = 11$	Ⓐ	Ⓑ
$? + 11 = 15$	Ⓒ	Ⓓ
$? = 15 + 11$	Ⓔ	Ⓕ
$11 + 15 = ?$	Ⓖ	Ⓗ

Performance Task

Answer the questions. Show all your work on separate paper.

Your school has asked you to read 20 books over the summer.

- You need to read 6 books about animals.

- You need to read 3 books about people.

- The rest of the books must be about places or hobbies.

- You need to read at least 1 book about places and at least 1 book about hobbies.

Make a plan about the books that you will read over the summer.

- Tell how many books you will read about places.

- Tell how many books you will read about hobbies.

- Explain why your summer reading plan makes sense.

REFLECT

Make an Argument How did you check to make sure your summer reading plan makes sense?

Draw or write to show examples for each term. Then draw or write to show other math words in the unit.

add to put together two or more quantities, to find the total of two or more numbers, or to find how many in all.

My Example

bar graph a data display in which bars are used to show the number of items in each category.

My Example

difference the result of subtraction.

My Example

equal sign a symbol that means *is the same value as*.

My Example

equation a mathematical statement that uses an equal sign (=) to show that two things have the same value.

My Example

fact family a group of related equations that use the same numbers, but in a different order and two different operation symbols. A fact family can show the relationship between addition and subtraction.

My Example

open number line a straight line with only the numbers important to a problem labeled.

My Example

picture graph a data display in which pictures are used to show data.

My Example

sum the result of addition.

My Example

unknown number a number that is missing or not known in a problem, and is often shown as a box or a symbol.

My Example

My Word: _____

_____

_____

My Example

My Word: _____

_____

_____

My Example

UNIT

2

Numbers
Within 100

Addition,
Subtraction,
Time, and Money

☑ SELF CHECK

Before starting this unit, check off the skills you know below. As you complete each lesson, see how many more skills you can check off!

I can . . .	Before	After
Add two-digit numbers.	☐	☐
Add tens and add ones.	☐	☐
Regroup ones as a ten and decompose a ten.	☐	☐
Subtract two-digit numbers.	☐	☐
Solve one-step and two-step word problems by adding or subtracting two-digit numbers.	☐	☐
Solve word problems involving money.	☐	☐
Tell and write time to the nearest 5 minutes.	☐	☐

Build Your Vocabulary

Math Vocabulary

Work with a partner to complete the table.

Review Words	What does it mean?	Your Example
hour		
making a ten		
tally mark		
teen number		

Academic Vocabulary

**Put a check next to the academic words you know.
Then use the words to complete the sentences.**

☐ check   ☐ decide   ☐ arrange   ☐ solution

1 Math is often used to find a .... to a problem in the real world.

2 After I solve a problem, I .... my work.

3 Before you tackle a problem, ... on a strategy to use.

4 Placing numbers in order from least to greatest is a

way to .... information.

Add Two-Digit Numbers

Dear Family,

This week your child is learning to use different strategies to add two-digit numbers.

Here are some ways to find the sum 28 + 47.

- Use base-ten blocks.

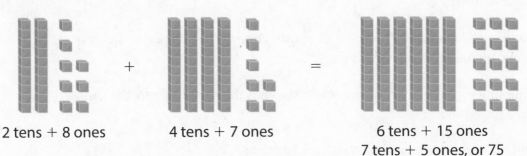

2 tens + 8 ones   4 tens + 7 ones   6 tens + 15 ones
7 tens + 5 ones, or 75

- Add tens and ones.

$$28 = 20 + 8$$
$$47 = \underline{40 + 7}$$
$$60 + 15 = 75$$

- Go to the next 10.
  It is easier to add when one number has no ones. To simplify adding, go to the next ten.

$28 + 2 = 30$
$30 + 40 = 70$
$70 + 5 = 75$
$28 + 47 = 75$

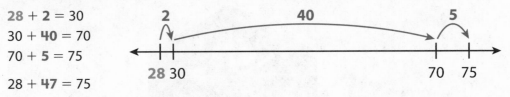

Invite your child to share what he or she knows about addition strategies by doing the following activity together.

ACTIVITY ADDITION STRATEGIES

Do this activity with your child to explore adding two-digit numbers.

Materials 2 number cubes, pencil, and paper

Explain to your child that the point of the game is to get a sum greater than 75.

- Have your child roll two number cubes.

- Ask your child to form a two-digit number from the number cubes
  (For example, if you roll a 2 and a 6, you can make 26 or 62.) Write the
  number down.

- Ask your child to add 25 to the number, using one of the addition strategies
  shown on the other side of this paper.

- If the sum is greater than 75, then he or she wins the round. Repeat the game
  three more times.

During the game, ask your child questions such as:

- *Does it matter which number you make with the two number cubes? Will you
  get the same sum either way?*

- *How can you pick the numbers to make sure your sum is as great as possible?*

- *What happens to my two-digit number if I use the greater digit in the tens place?
  In the ones place?*

Explore Adding Two-Digit Numbers

You know how to add one-digit numbers. Use what you know to try to solve the problem below.

> One day, Jack finds 27 cans to recycle.
> The next day, he finds 15 cans to recycle.
> How many cans does Jack find altogether?

TRY IT

Math Toolkit
- base-ten blocks
- open number lines
- tens place-value mats

DISCUSS IT

Ask your partner:
Why did you choose that strategy?

Tell your partner:
I started by . . .

CONNECT IT

① LOOK BACK

How many cans does Jack find altogether? ....

② LOOK AHEAD

Here are some ways to find $27 + 15$.

Use base-ten blocks.

a.

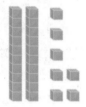 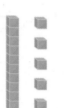 

2 tens and
7 ones

1 ten and
5 ones

.... tens and

.... ones

Go to the next ten.

b. $27 + 3 =$ ....

$30 + 10 =$ ....

$40 + 2 =$ ....

Add tens, then ones.

c.
$$\begin{array}{r} 20 \\ + 10 \\ \hline \end{array} \quad \begin{array}{r} 7 \\ + 5 \\ \hline \end{array}$$

.... $+$ .... $= 42$

③ REFLECT

Why is adding 3, 10, and 2 the same as adding 15?

....

....

Prepare for Adding Two-Digit Numbers

1 Think about what you know about adding numbers.
Fill in each box. Use words, numbers, and pictures.
Show as many ideas as you can.

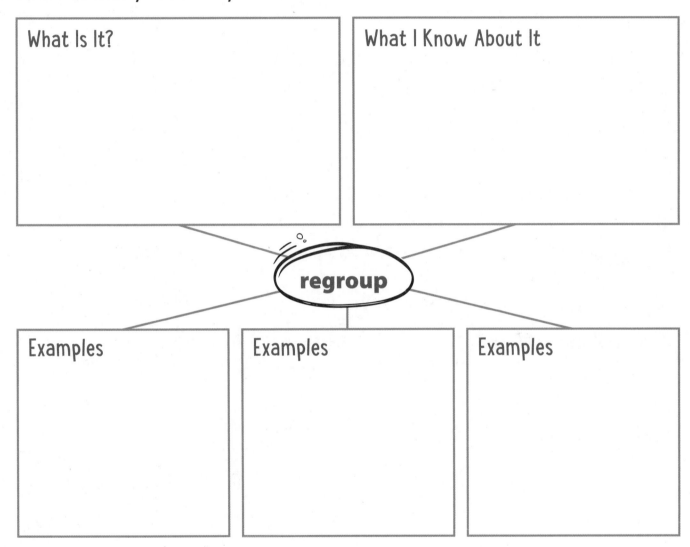

What Is It?

What I Know About It

regroup

Examples

Examples

Examples

2 Why is adding 6, 10, and 5 to a number the same as
adding 21 to that number?

3 Solve the problem. Show your work.

Nabila has 38 pennies. Her friend Manny gives her 17 pennies. How many pennies does Nabila have now?

Solution ....

4 Check your answer. Show your work.

Develop Different Ways to Show Addition

Read and try to solve the problem below.

> Before lunch, Maria reads for 38 minutes. After lunch, she reads for 45 minutes. How many total minutes does Maria read?

TRY IT

 **Math Toolkit**
- base-ten blocks
- open number lines

DISCUSS IT

Ask your partner: How did you get started?

Tell your partner: The strategy I used to find the answer was...

Explore different ways to understand and show adding two-digit numbers.

> Before lunch, Maria reads for 38 minutes. After lunch, she reads for 45 minutes. How many total minutes does Maria read?

PICTURE IT

You can use base-ten blocks.

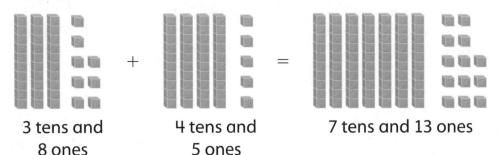

3 tens and   4 tens and   7 tens and 13 ones
8 ones   5 ones

MODEL IT

You can add tens and add ones.

$$38 = 30 + 8$$
$$45 = \underline{40 + 5}$$
$$70 + 13$$

MODEL IT

You can go to the next ten.

$$38 + 2 = 40$$
$$40 + 40 = 80$$
$$80 + 3 = ?$$

CONNECT IT

Now you will use the problem from the previous page to help you understand how to add tens and ones.

1 Look at **Picture It** on the previous page.
What is the total number of tens and ones?

.... tens + ... ones

2 How many tens and ones are in 13?

13 = ... ten and .... ones, or .... + 3.

3 Add both tens. Then add the ones.

70 + 10 + 3 = ... + ...

= ....

4 Explain how you would add 38 + 45.

5 REFLECT

Look back at your **Try It**, strategies by classmates, and **Picture It** and **Model Its**. Which models or strategies do you like best for showing addition? Explain.

....

....

....

APPLY IT

Use what you just learned to solve these problems.

6 Mr. Dane has 17 pens and 37 pencils. How many pens and pencils does he have in all? Show your work.

Solution ....

7 Explain how to go to the next ten to add 36 + 18. Show your work.

8 What is the sum of 67 and 19?

Ⓐ 76

Ⓑ 79

Ⓒ 86

Ⓓ 89

Practice Different Ways to Show Addition

Study the Example showing how to use base-ten blocks to add two-digit numbers. Then solve problems 1–7.

EXAMPLE

Find 18 + 24.

1 ten and   2 tens and   3 tens and
8 ones   4 ones   12 ones

3 tens 12 ones = 30 + 10 + 2
$$= 40 + 2$$
$$= 42$$

Max has 29 rocks. Then he finds 15 more rocks.

1   Write the tens and ones. Then add the tens and ones.

.... tens .... ones + ... ten .... ones = ... tens .... ones

2   How many tens and ones are in 14?

14 = ... ten and .... ones, or 10 + ...

3   Add the tens. Then add the ones.

30 + 10 + 4 = ... + ..., or ....

Max has .... rocks.

Ms. Kottler has 27 black pens and 14 blue pens.

4 Write the tens and ones.

$27 = 20 +$ ....

$14 =$ .... $+$ ....

5 Add the tens, then add the ones from problem 4.
How many pens does Ms. Kottler have in all?
Show your work.

.... pens

There are 36 girls with red shirts. There are 19 boys with red shirts. There are 16 girls with blue shirts.

6 How many girls are there? Show your work.

.... girls

7 How many children have red shirts? Show your work.

.... red shirts

Develop More Ways to Show Addition

Read and try to solve the problem below.

> **There are 48 students on Bus A and 43 students on Bus B. How many students are on both buses?**

TRY IT

 Math Toolkit
- base-ten blocks
- open number lines
- tens place-value mats

Bus A

Bus B

 **DISCUSS IT**

Ask your partner: Do you agree with me? Why or why not?

Tell your partner: A model I used was... It helped me because...

Explore more ways to understand and show addition.

> There are **48** students on Bus A and **43** students on Bus B. How many students are on both buses?

PICTURE IT

You can use a quick drawing.

Show each number with a quick drawing.

It is easier to add when one number has no ones.
So, **regroup** to make a ten.

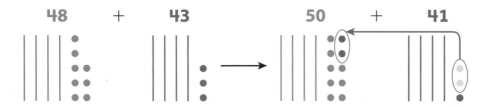

MODEL IT

You can use an open number line.

Start with **48**. Add **2** to go to the next ten.
To add **40**, count on by tens from 50: 60, 70, 80, 90.
Then add **1** more.

CONNECT IT

Now you will use the problem from the previous page to help you understand how to make a ten to add.

Look at **Picture It** on the previous page.

1 Why do you add 2 to 48?

2 What does the drawing show? Fill in the blanks.

$$48 \quad + \quad 43$$
$$+ \ \boxed{} \qquad - \ \boxed{}$$
$$\overline{\quad 50 \quad} + \quad \overline{\quad 41 \quad} = \boxed{}$$

Look at **Model It** on the previous page.

3 What number should you get if you add all the jumps? Why?

4 Where is the answer on this open number line?

5 REFLECT

Look back at your **Try It**, strategies by classmates, and **Picture It** and **Model It**. Which models or strategies do you like best for showing addition? Explain.

....

....

APPLY IT

Use what you just learned to solve these problems.

6 Sam drives 39 miles north. Then she drives 28 miles east. How far does she drive altogether? Show your work.

Solution ....

7 Find 23 + 37. Show your work.

23 + 37 = ...

8 Explain how the addition problem 17 + 48 could be solved by adding 20 + 45. Show your work.

Practice More Ways to Show Addition

Study the Example showing how to use quick drawings to add two-digit numbers. Then solve problems 1–6.

EXAMPLE

What is $37 + 24$?

$37 + 24$ is the same as $40 + 21$.

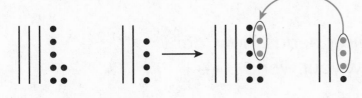

$40 + 21 = 61$

So, $37 + 24 = 61$.

Kim picks 28 apples. Nate picks 17 apples.

1 Look at the quick drawing. Then fill in the blanks.

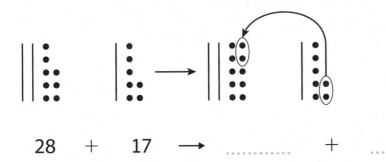

28   +   17   ⟶   ....   + ...

2 How many apples do Kim and Nate pick in all? ....

3 57 + 14 is the same as .... + ...

4 Fill in the missing numbers in the open number line. Then find 57 + 14.

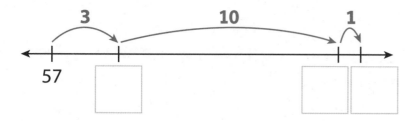

57 + 14 = ...

5 Mia has 49 red beads and 36 yellow beads. How many beads does Mia have in all? Show your work.

Solution ....

6 The equation below shows a sum of 51. Write three different equations with a sum of 51.

22 + 29 = 51

Refine Adding Two-Digit Numbers

Complete the Example below. Then solve problems 1–3.

EXAMPLE

Lucas has 47 rocks in his collection. He gets 34 more rocks. How many rocks does Lucas have now?

You can add tens and add ones.

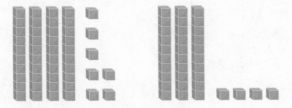

$40 + 30 = 70$
$7 + 4 = 11$, and $11 = 10 + 1$

How many rocks does Lucas have now? ....

APPLY IT

1 Blanca sells 59 flags at a parade. She has 37 flags left. How many flags did she have before the parade? Show your work.

How many tens are in each number? How many ones?

2 What is the sum of 47 and 28? Show your work.

> What can you add to 47 to get to the next ten?

Solution ....

3 Jenny gets 53 points in her first board game. She gets 38 points in her second game. What is the total number of points Jenny gets?

Ⓐ 81

Ⓑ 93

Ⓒ 91

Ⓓ 83

> Does it matter which number you start with?

Brady chose Ⓐ as the correct answer. How did Brady get his answer?

Practice Adding Two-Digit Numbers

1   Diego reads 48 pages of a book one day. The next day, he reads 23 pages. How many pages does Diego read in all?

> You can add the tens and add the ones.

Ⓐ 61

Ⓑ 62

Ⓒ 71

Ⓓ 75

2   Which addition problems could be solved by adding $40 + 15$?

> What do you add to one of the addends to get 40?

Ⓐ $39 + 16$

Ⓑ $38 + 13$

Ⓒ $37 + 18$

Ⓓ $36 + 17$

Ⓔ $35 + 19$

3   Tell if the equation can be used to solve $27 + 56$. Choose *Yes* or *No* for each problem.

> There are many ways to add two-digit numbers.

	Yes	No
$20 + 50 + 10 + 6 = 86$	Ⓐ	Ⓑ
$20 + 7 + 50 + 6 = 83$	Ⓒ	Ⓓ
$30 + 56 = 86$	Ⓔ	Ⓕ
$20 + 50 + 13 = 83$	Ⓖ	Ⓗ

4   A fruit salad has 37 green grapes and 45 red grapes. How many grapes are in the fruit salad?

Ⓐ 72

Ⓑ 81

Ⓒ 82

Ⓓ 712

Tim chose Ⓐ as the correct answer. How did Tim get his answer?

How many tens are you adding?

5   Dan has 29 books. Kayla has 3 more books than Dan. How many books do Dan and Kayla have altogether? Show your work.

How many books does Kayla have?

Solution

Refine Adding Two-Digit Numbers

APPLY IT

Solve the problems.

1 Which addition problems show a way to add $78 + 16$?

Ⓐ $70 + 8 + 10 + 6$

Ⓑ $70 + 10 + 8 + 6$

Ⓒ $80 + 14$

Ⓓ $70 + 8 + 6$

Ⓔ $70 + 10 + 6$

2 Jo does 36 sit-ups. Then she does 27 more. How many sit-ups does Jo do in all?

Ⓐ 67

Ⓑ 63

Ⓒ 53

Ⓓ 9

3 Tell if the equation shows how to find $24 + 9$.

Choose *Yes* or *No* for each problem.

	Yes	No
$20 + 4 + 9 = 33$	Ⓐ	Ⓑ
$2 + 4 + 9 = 15$	Ⓒ	Ⓓ
$20 + 40 + 9 = 69$	Ⓔ	Ⓕ
$20 + 10 + 3 = 33$	Ⓖ	Ⓗ

4 Ms. Ames shows her students the problem at the right. What did she do? Explain. Then show how to solve the problem a different way

$$
\begin{array}{r}
25 \\
+\ 59 \\
\hline
14 \\
+\ 70 \\
\hline
84
\end{array}
$$

5 Find $47 + 24$ the way Ms. Ames did in problem 4. Then show a different way. How do the sums compare?

6 MATH JOURNAL

What strategy would you use to solve $32 + 49$? Explain and then solve.

☑ SELF CHECK Go back to the Unit 2 Opener and see what you can check off.

Subtract Two-Digit Numbers

Dear Family,

This week your child is learning strategies for subtracting two-digit numbers.

Your child will be applying strategies to solve problems such as the one below.

Rex has 65 dollars. He spends 37 dollars. How much money does he have left?

- One strategy your child might use is called "adding up."
The subtraction equation $65 - 37 = ?$ shows the same relationship as the addition equation $37 + ? = 65$. You can think of this as: how much do you have to add to 37 to get to 65?
You can use an open number line to solve this.

$37 + \mathbf{20} = 57$
$57 + \mathbf{3} = 60$
$60 + \mathbf{5} = 65$
$\mathbf{20 + 3 + 5 = 28}$

So, $37 + 28 = 65$, and $65 - 37 = 28$.

- Another strategy you child might use is called "subtracting to make a ten." There are 7 ones in 37 but only 5 in 65, so start by subtracting 5. Then subtract the tens. Then subtract the rest of the ones (2).

$65 - \mathbf{5} = 60$
$60 - \mathbf{30} = 30$
$30 - \mathbf{2} = 28$
$\mathbf{65 - 37 = 28}$

Whichever strategy you use, you will get the same answer:
Rex has 28 dollars left.

Invite your child to share what he or she knows about subtracting by doing the following activity together.

ACTIVITY SUBTRACTION STRATEGIES

Do this activity with your child to explore subtracting two-digit numbers.

Make up a subtraction word problem using two-digit numbers you encounter in your everyday life. Use ideas like these:

1. *A dog weighs 27 pounds. A cat weighs 12 pounds. How much more does the dog weigh than the cat?*

2. *Your friend has saved 21 dollars. How much more does he need so he can buy that 49-dollar video game he's been wanting?*

3. *It is 65 miles from home to the water park and 78 miles from home to the amusement park. How much farther is it to the amusement park than to the water park?*

4. *The chapter book we are reading has 84 pages. We have read 55 pages. How many more pages do we have to read?*

Have your child write and solve an equation and then draw a picture to illustrate the word problem. You can also use a bar model to help you solve subtraction problems.

Answers: **1.** 15 pounds; **2.** 28 dollars; **3.** 13 miles; **4.** 29 pages

Explore Subtracting Two-Digit Numbers

You know how to subtract one-digit numbers. Use what you know to try to solve the problem below.

> There are 34 art projects in a contest. There are 9 paintings. The rest are drawings. How many art projects are drawings?

TRY IT

Math Toolkit
- connecting cubes
- base-ten blocks
- hundred charts
- open number lines
- bar models

DISCUSS IT

Ask your partner: How did you get started?

Tell your partner: I started by . . .

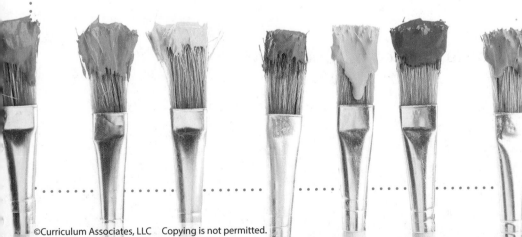

CONNECT IT

1 LOOK BACK

How many of the art projects are drawings? ....

2 LOOK AHEAD

Here are some ways to find 34 − 9.

a. Start at 9 and add up to 34.

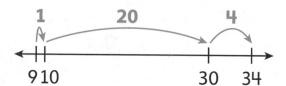

Go to the next 10.   9 + ... = 10

Add to get to 30.   10 + ... = 30

Add to get to 34.   30 + ... = 34

Total the jumps. ⟶ ....

9 + ... = 34, so 34 − 9 = ...

b. Subtract to make a ten.

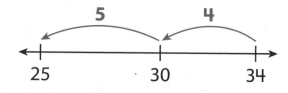

Subtract 4 first. Then subtract 5.

34 − 4 = 30

30 − 5 = 25

34 − 9 = ...

3 REFLECT

Why does the number line in problem 2b show a jump
of 4 and a jump of 5?

....

....

Prepare for Subtracting Two-Digit Numbers

1 Think about what you know about two-digit numbers. Fill in each box. Use words, numbers, and pictures. Show as many ideas as you can.

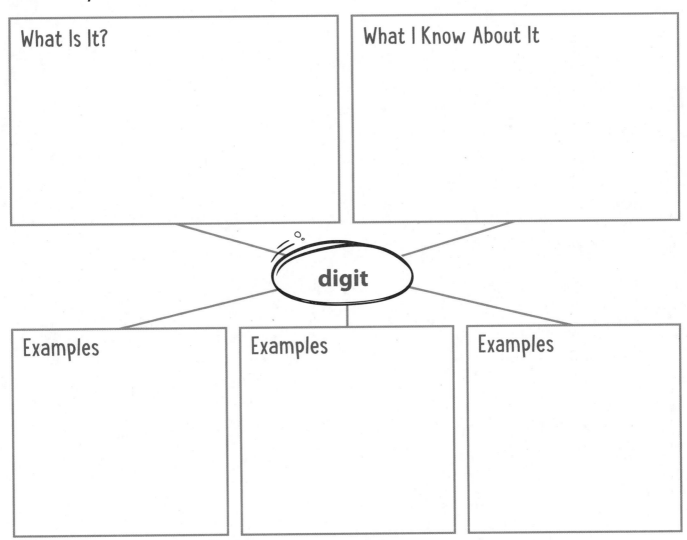

What Is It?

What I Know About It

digit

Examples

Examples

Examples

2 Which digit will change when you subtract 67 – 5? Explain.

3 Solve the problem. Show your work.

There are 22 chairs in the classroom. 7 of the chairs are made of wood. The rest are plastic. How many chairs are plastic?

Solution ....

4 Check your answer. Show your work.

Develop Subtracting by Adding Up

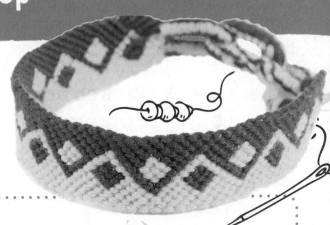

Read and try to solve the problem below.

> There are 54 children at camp. 27 are girls. How many boys are at camp?

TRY IT

🧰 **Math Toolkit**
- connecting cubes
- base-ten blocks ▶
- hundred charts
- open number lines ▶
- bar models

DISCUSS IT

Ask your partner:
Why did you choose that strategy?

Tell your partner:
The strategy I used to find the answer was . . .

Explore different ways to understand subtracting by adding up.

> There are 54 children at camp. 27 are girls. How many boys are at camp?

MODEL IT

You can add tens first.

$54 - 27 = ?$ is the same as $27 + ? = 54$.

27 + **20** = 47

47 + **3** = 50

50 + **4** = 54

20 + **3** + **4** = ?

MODEL IT

You can add up to the next ten.

$54 - 27 = ?$ is the same as $27 + ? = 54$.

Start with 27 and add 3.
Then add 20 to get to 50.
Finally, add 4 to get to 54.

27 + **3** = 30

30 + **20** = 50

50 + **4** = 54

3 + **20** + **4** = ?

You can count up by tens to add 20. Think: 40, 50.

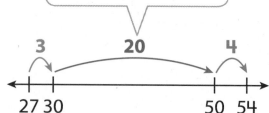

CONNECT IT

Now you will use the problem from the previous page to help you understand how to subtract by adding up.

1 Look at the first **Model It**.
What number do you start with? ....

What number do you stop at? ....

2 Look at the second **Model It**.
Why do you add 3 first?

3 What is 54 − 27? How did you get your answer?

4 How are the two models on the previous page alike?
How are they different?

5 REFLECT

Look back at your **Try It**, strategies by classmates, and **Model Its**. Which models or strategies do you like best for showing subtraction? Explain.

....

....

....

APPLY IT

Use what you just learned to solve these problems.

6 Subtract 71 − 36 by adding up. Show your work.

Solution ....

7 Explain how the subtraction problem 82 − 25 could be solved by adding tens first.

8 Teddy and Laura collect stamps. Teddy has 93 stamps and Laura has 76 stamps. How many more stamps does Teddy have than Laura?

Ⓐ 13 more stamps

Ⓑ 17 more stamps

Ⓒ 23 more stamps

Ⓓ 27 more stamps

Practice Subtracting by Adding Up

Study the Example that shows how to subtract two-digit numbers by adding up. Then solve problems 1–6.

EXAMPLE

A store has 82 hats. There are 45 blue hats. The rest are red. How many hats are red?

$82 - 45 = ?$ is the same as $45 + ? = 82$.

You can add tens first. Then add ones.

$45 + \mathbf{30} = 75$
$75 + \mathbf{5} = 80$
$80 + \mathbf{2} = 82$

30   5   2

```
←+————————————————————+——+—+→
 45                   75 80 82
```

$30 + 5 + 2 = 37$. There are 37 red hats in the store.

Mr. Kent needs 74 plates for a picnic. He has 28 plates. He will buy the rest of the plates he needs.

1 Show how you can find how many plates Mr. Kent needs to buy. Fill in the blanks to find $74 - 28$. Add tens first.

$28 + \rule{2cm}{0.4pt} = 68$

$68 + \rule{2cm}{0.4pt} = 70$

40   2 4

```
←+————————————————————+—+—+→
 28                  68 70 74
```

$70 + \rule{2cm}{0.4pt} = 74$

$40 + \rule{2cm}{0.4pt} + \rule{2cm}{0.4pt} = \rule{2cm}{0.4pt}$

2 How many plates should Mr. Kent buy?

$\rule{2cm}{0.4pt}$ plates

Ms. Jones has 54 pencils. She gives 17 of the pencils to her students. How many pencils does Ms. Jones have left?

3 Show how you can add ones first to find 54 − 17. Fill in the boxes on the number line.

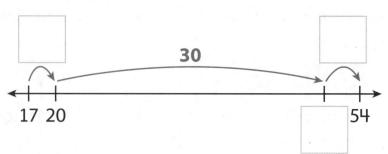

30

17 20   54

4 How many pencils does Ms. Jones have left?
Show your work.

Solution ....

There are 65 trees in the town park. 38 are apple trees. The rest are oak trees.

5 How many oak trees are there? Add up to find 65 − 38.
Show your work.

Solution ....

6 To solve problem 5, did you add tens or ones first?
Explain why.

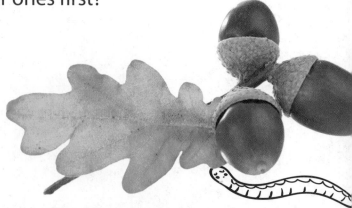

Develop Subtracting by Regrouping

Read and try to solve the problem below.

> Ming has 42 toy animals. She gives 15 animals to her friends. How many toy animals does Ming have left?

TRY IT

 **Math Toolkit**
- connecting cubes
- base-ten blocks
- hundred charts
- open number lines
- bar models

Explore different ways to understand subtracting by regrouping.

> **Ming has 42 toy animals. She gives 15 animals to her friends. How many toy animals does Ming have left?**

MODEL IT
You can regroup a ten first and then subtract.

Find 42 − 15.

42 = 3 tens and 12 ones

First regroup.
Make 10 ones
with 1 ten in 42.

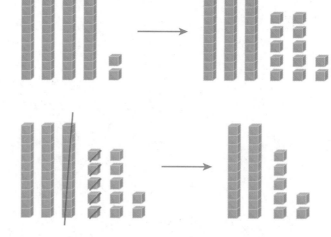

Then subtract.

    3 tens and 12 ones
  − 1 ten and   5 ones

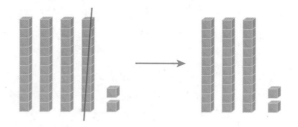

MODEL IT
You can subtract tens first.

Find 42 − 15.

Subtract a ten.
15 = 1 ten and 5 ones.

Take away 1 ten.

    42 − 10 = 32

Then regroup.
Make 10 ones with 1 ten.
Then take away 5 ones.

CONNECT IT

Now you will use the problem from the previous page to help you understand how to subtract by regrouping.

1 Look at the first **Model It**. Why do you make 10 ones with 1 ten in 42?

2 How many tens and ones are left after

you subtract? .... tens and .... ones

3 Look at the second **Model It**. How many tens and ones are left after you subtract the ten

and the 5 ones? .... tens and .... ones

4 Why do both **Model Its** give the same answer?

5 REFLECT

Look back at your **Try It**, strategies by classmates, and the **Model Its**. Which models or strategies do you like best for showing subtraction? Explain.

....

....

....

....

APPLY IT

Use what you just learned about subtracting by regrouping to solve these problems.

6 Subtract 82 − 63 by taking away tens and ones. Show your work.

Solution ....

7 Solve this problem. Show your work.

Anna has 63 pennies. She spends 28 pennies. How many pennies does she have now?

Solution ....

8 Find 52 − 19.

Ⓐ 61

Ⓑ 47

Ⓒ 43

Ⓓ 33

Practice Subtracting by Regrouping

Study the Example showing how to subtract two-digit numbers by regrouping a ten. Then solve problems 1–6.

EXAMPLE

What is 33 − 18?
You can regroup a ten first.
Then subtract.

33 = 2 tens and 13 ones

$$
\begin{array}{r}
2 \text{ tens and } 13 \text{ ones} \\
- \; 1 \text{ ten and } 8 \text{ ones} \\
\hline
1 \text{ ten and } 5 \text{ ones} = 15
\end{array}
$$

33 − 18 = 15

Kate paints 44 stars. She paints 27 of the stars silver. She paints the rest gold.

1 Regroup a ten in 44. Fill in the blank.

44 = 3 tens and .... ones

2 How many stars are gold? Find 44 − 27. Show your work.

Solution .... stars are gold.

3 Subtract tens first to solve 51 − 22. Fill in the blanks.

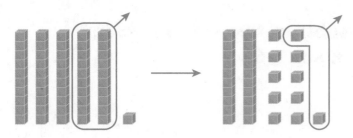

51 − .... = 31   31 − .... = ...

4 Wyatt solves 57 − 38. He subtracts tens first. Fill in the blanks to show the next step and the answer.

57 − 30 = 27   27 − .... = ...

5 There are 32 boys and girls on the playground. There are 19 girls. How many boys are on the playground? Show your work.

Solution ....

6 Dora finds 73 − 26. Fill in the blanks to finish her subtraction.

73 − 3 = ...

70 − .... = 50

.... − .... = ...

Refine Subtracting Two-Digit Numbers

Complete the Example below. Then solve problems 1–3.

EXAMPLE

Joe has 52 cards. He puts 28 cards in one pile and the rest in a second pile. How many cards are in the second pile? Find 52 − 28.

You can show your work on an open number line.

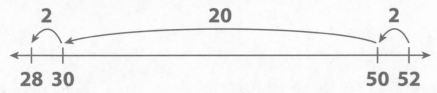

Jump down 2 + 20 + 2, or 24, to get to 28.
So, 52 − 28 = 24.

Solution ....

APPLY IT

1 At the farm, there are 92 fruit trees. Of these, 69 are apple trees. The rest are pear trees. How many pear trees are there? Find 92 − 69. Show your work.

> If you add up, what number do you start with?

Solution ....

2 Corey says that the difference of 54 and 38 is 22. He shows his work on the open number line below.

What does each jump show?

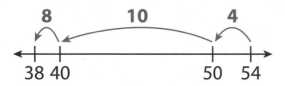

His friend says his answer is not correct. What should Corey do to fix his work?

3 Pedro does 57 jumping jacks. Ray does 18 fewer jumping jacks than Pedro. How many jumping jacks does Ray do?

Ⓐ 29

Ⓑ 39

Ⓒ 40

Ⓓ 41

How many do you take away from 57 to make a ten?

Mia chose Ⓒ as the correct answer. How did Mia get her answer?

Practice Subtracting Two-Digit Numbers

1 There are 54 children in a parade. There are 15 holding flags. The rest play instruments. How many children play instruments? Find $54 - 15$. Show your work.

> I can add up to subtract. Which number do I start with?

Solution ....

2 Show another way to find $54 - 15$. Make sure it is different than what you did in problem 1.

> You can regroup a ten first. You can also subtract tens first.

3 Choose *Yes* or *No* to tell if you can use the equations to find $43 - 26$.

> How many tens and ones are in 26?

	Yes	No
$26 + 4 = 30$ and $30 + 13 = 43$	Ⓐ	Ⓑ
$26 + 10 = 36$ and $36 + 3 = 39$	Ⓒ	Ⓓ
$43 - 10 = 33$ and $33 - 6 = 27$	Ⓔ	Ⓕ
$43 - 20 = 23$ and $23 - 6 = 17$	Ⓖ	Ⓗ

4 There are 86 cars in the parking lot. Then 37 cars drive away. How many cars are in the parking lot now? Find 86 − 37.

Ⓐ 59

Ⓑ 56

Ⓒ 49

Ⓓ 43

How can you write 86 so that you have 16 ones?

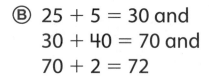

5 Which of the strategies below could help you find 72 − 25? Select all the correct answers.

Ⓐ 72 − 30 = 42 and
42 − 5 = 37

Ⓑ 25 + 5 = 30 and
30 + 40 = 70 and
70 + 2 = 72

What methods do you know for subtracting two-digit numbers?

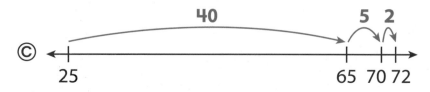

Ⓒ

Ⓓ   6 tens   12 ones
 − 2 tens   5 ones

Ⓔ 72 − 50 = 22 and
22 − 5 = 17

Refine Subtracting Two-Digit Numbers

APPLY IT

Solve the problems.

1 What is 35 − 17? Show your work.

Solution ....

2 Jamie draws the model below to solve a problem. Which problem does she solve?

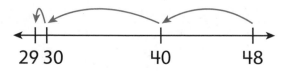

29 30   40   48

Ⓐ 40 − 11 = 29

Ⓑ 48 − 18 = 29

Ⓒ 48 − 18 = 30

Ⓓ 48 − 19 = 29

3 Don has 32 shells. He gives 15 to his brother. How many shells does Don have now? Show two ways to find 32 − 15.

4 Choose *Yes* or *No* to tell if you can use the strategy to find 56 − 17.

	Yes	No
56 − 6 = 50 and 50 − 1 = 49	Ⓐ	Ⓑ
56 − 10 = 46 and 46 − 7 = 39	Ⓒ	Ⓓ
17 + 3 = 20 and 20 + 36 = 56	Ⓔ	Ⓕ
4 tens and 16 ones − 1 ten and 7 ones ————————————— 3 tens and 9 ones	Ⓖ	Ⓗ

5 Greg subtracts 73 − 44. Fill in the blanks to finish his subtraction.

73 − 40 = ...

33 − .... = 30

.... − .... = ...

6 MATH JOURNAL

What strategy would you use to solve 82 − 58? Explain and then solve.

☑ SELF CHECK Go back to the Unit 2 Opener and see what you can check off.

Use Addition and Subtraction Strategies with Two-Digit Numbers

Dear Family,

This week your child is learning more strategies for adding and subtracting two-digit numbers.

Consider the following problem: *Sandy has 65 buttons. 27 of them are red and the rest of them are blue. How many blue buttons does Sandy have?*

- One strategy is to draw tens and ones. Use lines for tens and dots for ones.

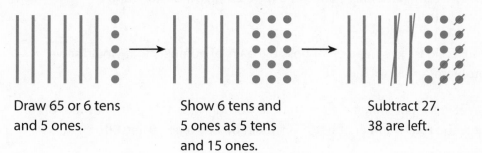

Draw 65 or 6 tens and 5 ones.

Show 6 tens and 5 ones as 5 tens and 15 ones.

Subtract 27. 38 are left.

- Another strategy is to "add up." The subtraction equation $65 - 27 = ?$ can be solved by thinking about $27 + ? = 65$.

$27 + 3 = 30$
$30 + 30 = 60$
$60 + 5 = 65$
$3 + 30 + 5 = 38$

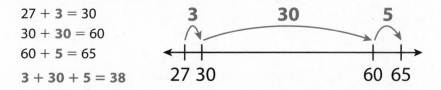

Whichever strategy you choose, you will get the same answer.
Sandy has 38 blue buttons.

You can check the answer to your subtraction problem by using addition.

Invite your child to share what he or she knows about using addition and subtraction strategies with two-digit numbers by doing the following activity together.

ACTIVITY USING ADDITION AND SUBTRACTION STRATEGIES WITH TWO-DIGIT NUMBERS

Do this activity with your child to use addition and subtraction strategies with two-digit numbers.

- Consider this problem: *Juan has a collection of 45 buttons. Some of them are yellow and some of them are green. How many buttons of each color could Juan have?*

- Explain to your child that there are many possible answers for this problem. One possible answer is that Juan could have 25 yellow buttons and 20 green buttons.

- Ask your child to give three other possible pairs of numbers that would solve this problem.

- Repeat at least four more times, each time starting with a different number of buttons. The total number of buttons should be between 30 and 80.

Look for real-life opportunities to solve problems with your child by using addition and subtraction strategies with two-digit numbers.

Explore Using Addition and Subtraction Strategies with Two-Digit Numbers

You know how to add and subtract two-digit numbers. Use what you know to try to solve the problem below.

> **Elizabeth has 35 toy cars. How can she put her toy cars on the top and bottom shelves of her bookcase? Show three ways.**

TRY IT

🧰 **Math Toolkit**
- connecting cubes
- base-ten blocks
- hundred charts
- bar models
- open number lines

DISCUSS IT

Ask your partner: How did you get started?

Tell your partner: I started by . . .

CONNECT IT

1 LOOK BACK

What are three ways that Elizabeth can put her toy cars on the top and bottom shelves of the bookcase?

2 LOOK AHEAD

You can use different strategies to solve addition and subtraction problems. Think about this problem.

Gary has 50 marbles. What are some different ways he can put them all into two bags?

Complete the equations to show three different ways.

.... + ... = 50

50 − .... = ...

50 = ... + ...

3 REFLECT

Are there other ways Gary could put the marbles into the two bags? Explain.

....

....

Prepare for Using Addition and Subtraction Strategies

1) Think about what you know about different ways to add and subtract. Fill in each box. Use words, numbers, and pictures. Show as many ideas as you can.

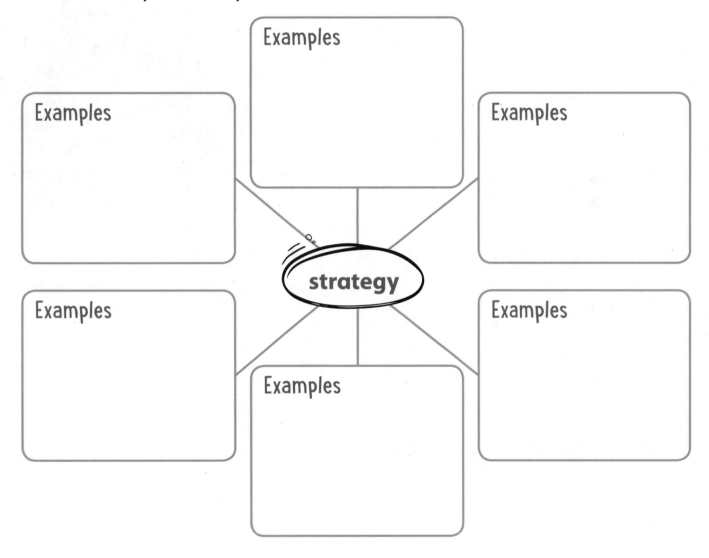

Examples

Examples

Examples

Examples

Examples

Examples

strategy

2) Clark solves ? − 23 = 19 by counting up on a number line. Did he use his strategy correctly? Explain.

19   20   23

3 Solve the problem. Show your work.

Diana has 42 dolls. How can she put her dolls on the top and bottom shelves of her bookcase? Show three ways.

Solution ....

....

....

4 Check your answer. Show your work.

Develop Strategies to Find a Missing Addend

Use what you know to try to solve the problem below.

> At the fair 39 students wait in line for a ride. Then some more students join the line. Now there are 93 students in line. How many more students join the line?

TRY IT

 Math Toolkit
- connecting cubes
- base-ten blocks
- hundred charts
- bar models
- open number lines

DISCUSS IT

Ask your partner:
Can you explain that again?

Tell your partner:
I am not sure how to find the answer because . . .

Develop different ways to find a missing addend.

At the fair 39 students wait in line for a ride. Then some more students join the line. Now there are 93 students in line. How many more students join the line?

MODEL IT

You can use an open number line.

Start at 39.
Add tens until you reach 89.
Next, **add 1** to reach 90.
Then **add 3** more ones to reach 93.

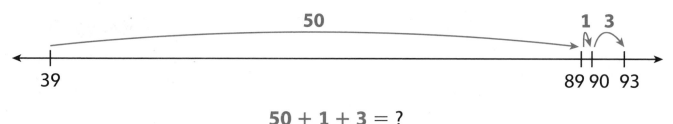

$$50 + 1 + 3 = ?$$

MODEL IT

You can add up to the next ten.

$39 + 1 = 40$

$40 + 50 = 90$

$90 + 3 = 93$

$1 + 50 + 3 = ?$

CONNECT IT

Now you will solve the problem from the previous page to help you understand strategies for adding two-digit numbers.

1 Look at the first **Model It** on the previous page.

What is $50 + 1 + 3$? ....

2 Look at the second **Model It** on the previous page.

What is $1 + 50 + 3$? ....

3 Why are your answers the same for problems 1 and 2?

4 Explain how you would find the missing addend in the equation below.

$$? + 47 = 83$$

5 REFLECT

Look back at your **Try It**, strategies by classmates, and **Model Its**. Which models or strategies do you like best for finding a missing addend? Explain.

....

....

APPLY IT

Use what you just learned to solve these problems.

6 Ricardo has 55 stamps. He gets some new stamps. Now Ricardo has 82 stamps. How many stamps does he get? Show your work.

Solution ....

7 Solve the problem by going to the next ten.

$58 + ? = 95$

Show your work.

Solution ....

8 Lee finds some seashells on Monday. He finds 31 seashells on Tuesday. Over the two days he finds 60 seashells. How many seashells does Lee find on Monday?

Ⓐ 23

Ⓑ 29

Ⓒ 90

Ⓓ 91

Practice Strategies to Find a Missing Addend

Study the Example showing how to use base-ten blocks to find a missing addend. Then solve problems 1–5.

EXAMPLE

Ms. Acosta's class reads 41 books in February and March. They read 17 of the books in February. How many books do they read in March?

Find $17 + ? = 41$.

$$17 + 24 = 41$$

Ms. Acosta's class reads 24 books in March.

Danny has $26. His parents give him some money for his birthday. Then he has $51. How much money do his parents give him?

1 Draw base-ten blocks for 26 in one color. Then use a different color to draw more base-ten blocks so that you have 51.

2 How many more blocks did you draw? ....

How much money do Danny's parents give him? $ ....

3 Chen hikes some miles during the first week of his vacation. During the second week of his vacation, he hikes 18 miles. He hikes 37 miles total during both weeks. How many miles does Chen hike during the first week? Show your work.

Solution ....

4 A bakery sells 48 muffins in the morning. Some of the muffins are blueberry and the rest of the muffins are cherry. Which equations show how many of each type of muffin the bakery could sell?

Ⓐ $48 = 47 + 1$

Ⓑ $30 + 18 = 48$

Ⓒ $24 + 24 = 48$

Ⓓ $48 + 12 = 60$

Ⓔ $48 = 14 + 34$

5 Nirupa adds to the next ten to find $65 + 25$. Tell how she might find the sum. Show your work.

Develop Using Subtraction Strategies with Two-Digit Numbers

Use what you know to try to solve the problem below.

> After school 85 students go home.
> Some of the students go home on a bus,
> but 26 students do not go home on a bus.
> How many students go home on a bus?

TRY IT

 **Math Toolkit**
- connecting cubes
- base-ten blocks
- hundred charts
- bar models
- open number lines

DISCUSS IT

Ask your partner:
Why did you choose that strategy?

Tell your partner:
The strategy I used to find the answer was . . .

Develop different ways to understand subtraction strategies with two-digit numbers.

> **After school 85 students go home.**
> **Some of the students go home on a bus,**
> **but 26 students do not go home on a bus.**
> **How many students go home on a bus?**

MODEL IT

You can regroup a ten first and then subtract.

Find 85 − ? = 26.

85 − ? = 26 is the same as 85 − 26 = ?.

85 is 7 tens and 15 ones.

First make 10 ones with 1 ten in 85.

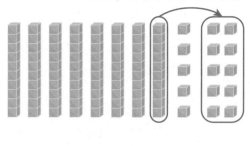

Then subtract.

$$
\begin{array}{r}
7 \text{ tens} \text{ and } 15 \text{ ones} \\
- \quad 2 \text{ tens} \text{ and } \ 6 \text{ ones} \\
\hline
\end{array}
$$

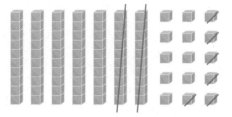

MODEL IT

You can use an open number line.

Subtract 26 from 85 to find how many students go home on a bus.

Start at 85. Subtract **5** to the next ten.
Next, subtract **1** more. Then subtract **20**.

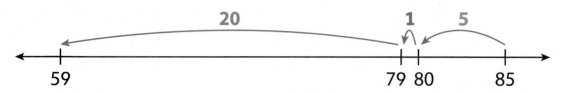

CONNECT IT

Now you will use the problem from the previous page to help you understand strategies to subtract two-digit numbers.

1 Look at the first **Model It**. What is 7 tens and 15 ones minus 2 tens and 6 ones?

2 Look at the second **Model It**.

What number did you land on? ....

3 Why are your answers the same for problems 1 and 2?

4 Explain how you can use addition to make sure your solution for $85 - ? = 26$ is correct.

5 REFLECT

Look back at your **Try It**, strategies by classmates, and **Model Its**. Which models or strategies do you like best for subtracting two-digit numbers? Explain.

....

....

....

APPLY IT

Use what you just learned to solve these problems.

6 There are 65 cherries in a bowl. Dan eats 12 cherries with his lunch. How many cherries are in the bowl now?

Use two different strategies to solve this problem. Show your work.

Solution ....

7 Look at how Kate solves a subtraction problem at the right. Is her answer correct? Explain how you can use addition to check her answer.

$$\begin{array}{r} 86 \\ -\ 58 \\ \hline 38 \end{array}$$

8 Sean has 14 fewer crayons than Keisha. Keisha has 64 crayons. How many crayons does Sean have?

Ⓐ 78

Ⓑ 60

Ⓒ 54

Ⓓ 50

Practice Using Subtraction Strategies with Two-Digit Numbers

Study the Example showing one way to subtract two-digit numbers. Then solve problems 1–4.

EXAMPLE

75 people are at a baseball game. 28 of the people are adults. The rest are children. How many children are at the baseball game?

$75 - 28 = ?$

Count back.

$75 - 5 = 70$
$70 - 20 = 50$
$50 - 3 = 47$

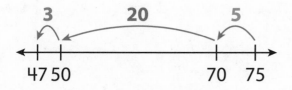

So, 47 children are at the baseball game.

Dave scores 43 points in a game and Lily scores 28. How many more points does Dave score than Lily?

1   Use an open number line to solve the problem.
    Show your work.

⟵──────────────────⟶

Solution ....

2 Which equations can you use to check if this subtraction equation is correct?

$72 - 24 = 48$

Ⓐ $72 + 24 = 96$

Ⓑ $48 + 48 = 96$

Ⓒ $48 + 24 = 72$

Ⓓ $72 - 48 = 24$

Ⓔ $24 + 48 = 72$

3 Show two different ways that you can use a number line to find $70 - 56$.

4 Which of the two number line strategies you used to solve problem 3 do you like best? Explain.

Refine Using Addition and Subtraction Strategies with Two-Digit Numbers

Complete the Example below. Then solve problems 1–3.

EXAMPLE

Two numbers have a sum of 80. What could the two numbers be? Write addition equations to show three possible pairs of numbers.

You can use any two numbers that have a sum of 80.

$20 + 60 = 80$

$80 = 45 + 35$

$50 + 30 = 80$

Solution ....

....

APPLY IT

1 Show a related subtraction equation for each of the addition equations shown in the Example.

$80 - \text{.........} = \text{.........}$

$80 - \text{.........} = \text{.........}$

$\text{.........} = 80 - \text{.........}$

How are addition and subtraction related?

2 A store has 57 granola bars. Then some of the granola bars are sold. Now there are 29 granola bars left. How many granola bars are sold? Show your work.

> Will you add or subtract to solve this problem?

Solution ....

3 Lisa sells 24 fewer tickets than Brad for the school's Fun Fair. Lisa sells 50 tickets. How many tickets does Brad sell?

> If Lisa sells fewer tickets than Brad, who sells more tickets?

Ⓐ 74

Ⓑ 64

Ⓒ 26

Ⓓ 16

Tyler chose Ⓒ as the correct answer. How did Tyler get his answer?

Practice Using Addition and Subtraction Strategies

1 Carmen has 53 animal cards. David has 29 animal cards. How many fewer cards does David have than Carmen? Show your work.

Do you need to add or subtract to solve this problem?

Solution ....

2 For problem 1 above, find how many more animal cards Carmen has than David.

How are problems 1 and 2 alike?

Carmen has .... more animal cards than David.

What do you notice about your answers for problems 1 and 2? Explain.

3 Choose *Yes* or *No* to tell if you can use the equations to solve for ? in the problem below.

$$? - 23 = 61$$

	Yes	**No**
$61 - ? = 23$	Ⓐ	Ⓑ
$23 + 61 = ?$	Ⓒ	Ⓓ
$61 - 23 = ?$	Ⓔ	Ⓕ
$? - 61 = 23$	Ⓖ	Ⓗ

How are the numbers in the equation related?

4 Of the 83 students on a field trip, 47 are girls. How many boys are on the field trip? Write an addition equation and a subtraction equation that can be used to find the solution.

How are addition and subtraction related?

5 During one month, Lily rides her bike 18 more miles than Raj. Lily rides her bike 50 miles. How many miles does Raj ride his bike?

Ⓐ 68

Ⓑ 48

Ⓒ 42

Ⓓ 32

If Lily rides more miles than Raj, then who rides fewer miles?

Cindy chose Ⓐ as the correct answer.

How did Cindy get her answer?

Refine Using Addition and Subtraction Strategies with Two-Digit Numbers

APPLY IT

Solve the problems.

1 Dalila makes this model to solve a problem. What problem does she solve? Write an equation.

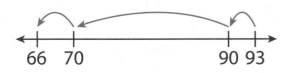

.... − .... = ...

2 A farmer has 76 horses. There are 27 horses inside the barn. The rest are outside. How many horses are outside?

Tell if you use the equation to solve the problem.

	Yes	No
$27 + ? = 76$	Ⓐ	Ⓑ
$76 = ? + 27$	Ⓒ	Ⓓ
$76 + 27 = ?$	Ⓔ	Ⓕ
$76 - 27 = ?$	Ⓖ	Ⓗ

3 Tim takes $75 to the store to buy some clothes. When he leaves the store, he has $19. How much does Tim spend at the store?

Ⓐ $56   Ⓑ $66

Ⓒ $84   Ⓓ $94

4 Ahmed and Jenna pick up cans. Yesterday, Ahmed picked up 18 more cans than Jenna. Ahmed picked up 47 cans.

Part A How many cans did Jenna pick up?
Show your work.

Jenna picked up .... cans.

Part B Today Jenna picks up 51 cans. How many more cans does Jenna pick up today than yesterday?
Show your work.

Jenna picks up .... more cans today than yesterday.

5 MATH JOURNAL

Show one of the strategies used in Part A or Part B in problem 4 with a model or quick drawing.

☑ SELF CHECK Go back to the Unit 2 Opener and see what you can check off.

Solve Word Problems with Two-Digit Numbers

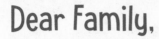

Dear Family,

This week your child is learning to solve one-step problems by adding and subtracting two-digit numbers.

Consider this word problem: *Jacinda has 15 pieces of sea glass in her collection. She goes to the beach and collects some more, and now she has 32 pieces of sea glass. How many pieces of sea glass does Jacinda collect at the beach?*

You can think of problems like this as you **start** with a number, **change** happens, and you end with a **total**. To solve the problem above, you need to find the change that happens.

This can be modeled in different ways to help write and solve equations.

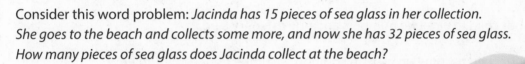

See how you can use a bar model to represent and solve the problem at the top of the page.

$$15 + ? = 32$$
$$32 - 15 = ?$$
$$32 - 15 = 17$$

Jacinda collects 17 pieces of sea glass at the beach.

Invite your child to share what he or she knows about solving one-step problems by doing the following activity together.

ACTIVITY SOLVING WORD PROBLEMS WITH TWO-DIGIT NUMBERS

Do this activity with your child to solve word problems with two-digit numbers.

Materials pen and paper, index cards (optional), scissors (optional)

- Help your child to create word problem cards by cutting out the prompts below or writing the prompts on index cards.

- Ask your child to pick two numbers and one category card.

- Ask your child to come up with an addition or subtraction word problem involving the numbers and category. For example, if your child chose 25, 42, and *pencils,* he or she might say: *Mike has 42 pencils and buys 25 more pencils. How many pencils does he have now?*

- Then ask your child to solve the word problem he or she created.

- Work with your child to create and solve 5 more word problems, picking combinations of numbers and categories each time.

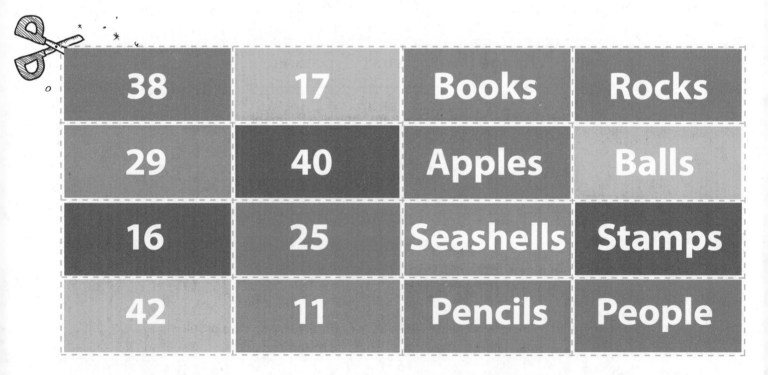

38	17	Books	Rocks
29	40	Apples	Balls
16	25	Seashells	Stamps
42	11	Pencils	People

Explore Solving Word Problems with Two-Digit Numbers

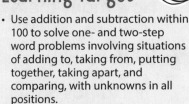

You know how to solve word problems with one-digit numbers. Use what you know to try to solve the problem below.

> **Mr. Soto's students can trade 75 milk caps for school supplies. They have 49 milk caps. How many more do they need to get to 75?**

Learning Target

- Use addition and subtraction within 100 to solve one- and two-step word problems involving situations of adding to, taking from, putting together, taking apart, and comparing, with unknowns in all positions.

SMP 1, 2, 3, 4, 5, 6, 8

TRY IT

Math Toolkit
- connecting cubes
- base-ten blocks 🖑
- bar models
- hundred charts
- open number lines 🖑

DISCUSS IT

Ask your partner: How did you get started?

Tell your partner: At first, I thought . . .

CONNECT IT

1 LOOK BACK

How many more milk caps does the class need? ....

2 LOOK AHEAD

Marta has 38 stickers. Tia gives her more stickers. Now Marta has 93 stickers. How many stickers does Tia give to Marta?

a. You can use a model to help find how many stickers Tia gives Marta. Complete the model.

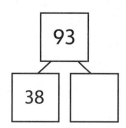

b. You can also use equations to show how many stickers Tia gives Marta. Complete the equations.

$38 +$ .... $= 93$ $93 - 38 =$ ....

3 REFLECT

Explain how you find the number of stickers Tia starts with if she has 27 left now.

....

....

....

Prepare for Solving Word Problems with Two-Digit Numbers

1. Think about what you know about word problems.
   Fill in each box. Use words, numbers, and pictures.
   Show as many ideas as you can.

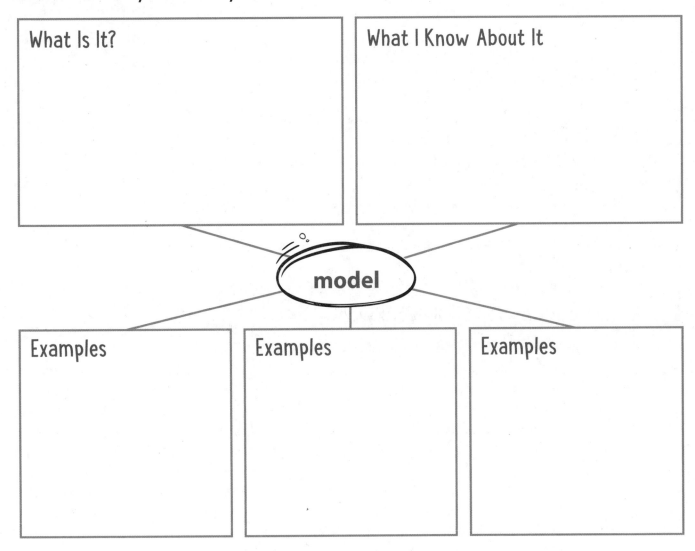

What Is It?	What I Know About It

model

Examples	Examples	Examples

2. Elena has 43 marbles. She gives 17 marbles to her friend. Does the model at the right help her find how many marbles she has left? Why or why not?

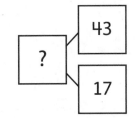

3 Solve the problem. Show your work.

Drew needs 55 bar codes to enter a contest. He has 32 bar codes. How many more bar codes does he need to get to 55?

Solution ....

4 Check your answer. Show your work.

Develop Ways to Model Word Problems

Read and try to solve the problem below.

Todd plays a game. The table shows his points.

Level 1	?
Level 2	16 points
Total	55 points

How many points does Todd get in Level 1?

TRY IT

Math Toolkit
- base-ten blocks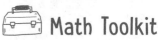
- number bonds
- bar models
- hundred charts
- open number lines

DISCUSS IT

Ask your partner:
Can you explain that again?

Tell your partner:
The strategy I used to find the answer was . . .

Explore different ways to understand modeling word problems.

Todd plays a game. The table shows his points.

Level 1	?
Level 2	16 points
Total	55 points

How many points does Todd get in Level 1?

PICTURE IT
You can draw a bar model.

55

?	16

MODEL IT
You can use an addition equation.

Level 1 Score	+	Level 2 Score	=	Total Score
?	+	16	=	55

MODEL IT
You can use a subtraction equation.

Total Score	−	Level 2 Score	=	Level 1 Score
55	−	16	=	?

CONNECT IT
Now you will use the problem from the previous page to help you understand how to model word problems.

1 Look at the second **Model It**. Write a different subtraction equation that you could use to solve the problem.

.... − .... = ...

2 Show how to solve the problem from the previous page on an open number line. Then write your answer.

Solution ....

3 How did you make your number line in problem 2? What is another way to find the answer?

4 REFLECT

Look back at your **Try It**, strategies by classmates, and **Picture It** and **Model Its**. Which models or strategies do you like best for modeling a word problem? Explain.

....

....

....

Lesson 9 Solve Word Problems with Two-Digit Numbers   **219**

APPLY IT

Use what you just learned to solve these problems.

5 Matt has 72 sports cards. Then he buys more cards. Now he has 90 cards. How many more cards does Matt buy? Show your work.

Solution ....

6 Neve has some flowers. Then she picks 18 more flowers. Now she has 43 flowers. How many flowers does Neve have at the start? Show your work.

Solution ....

7 Shari has a new camera. She takes 27 pictures on Monday. She takes 35 pictures on Tuesday. Which equations could you solve to find how many pictures Shari takes on the two days?

Ⓐ ? = 27 + 35

Ⓑ ? = 35 − 27

Ⓒ ? = 35 + 27

Ⓓ ? − 35 = 27

Ⓔ 35 − ? = 27

Practice Ways to Model Word Problems

Study the Example showing how to use equations to solve word problems. Then solve problems 1–6.

EXAMPLE

Ted has some beads. Then he gets 18 more beads. Now Ted has 42 beads. How many beads does Ted have to begin with?

Use addition: or   **Use subtraction:**

start + change = total   **total − change = start**

  ? + 18 = 42   42 − 18 = ?

? = 24

Ted has 24 beads to begin with.

Mrs. Tate has some fish in her fish tank. She buys 25 more fish. Now there are 73 fish in the fish tank.

1. Complete the model and the equations to show how many fish are in the fish tank at the start.

? + ... = ...

.... − .... = ?

2. How many fish are in the fish tank at the start? Show your work.

Solution ....

Mrs. Lopez drives a number of miles north. Then she drives 34 miles west. She drives 93 miles in all.

3 Complete the equations to show how many miles Mrs. Lopez drives north.

? + ... = ... and .... − .... = ?

4 Complete the open number line. Then solve the problem. Show your work.

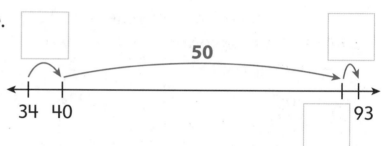

50

34   40   93

Mrs. Lopez drives .... miles north.

Stella has some cards. Then she makes 13 more cards. Now she has 41 cards.

5 How many cards does Stella start with? Show your work.

Solution ....

6 Write and solve a problem like problem 5. Use different numbers.

Develop More Ways to Model Word Problems

Read and try to solve the problem below.

> **Some books are on a shelf. Students take 24 books from the shelf. Then there are 38 books on the shelf. How many books are on the shelf to begin with?**

TRY IT

 Math Toolkit
- base-ten blocks
- number bonds
- bar models
- hundred charts
- open number lines

DISCUSS IT

Ask your partner: How did you choose that strategy?

Tell your partner: I disagree with this part because . . .

Explore more ways to understand modeling
word problems.

> Some books are on a shelf. Students take
> 24 books from the shelf. Then there are 38 books
> on the shelf. How many books are on the shelf to
> begin with?

MODEL IT

You can show the problem with words.

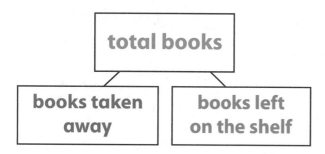

MODEL IT

You can show the problem with numbers.

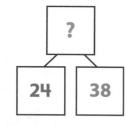

CONNECT IT

Now you will use the problem from the previous page to help you understand more ways to model and solve word problems.

1 Look at the second **Model It**. Write an addition equation and a subtraction equation for the problem.

.... = ... + ... − .... = ...

2 Write a different addition equation that you could use to solve the problem.

.... + ... = ...

3 What is the total number of books on the shelf to begin with? Show your work.

4 REFLECT

Look back at your **Try It**, strategies by classmates, and **Model Its**. Which models or strategies do you like best for modeling word problems? Explain.

....

....

....

....

APPLY IT

Use what you just learned to solve these problems.

5 Students help clean the park. At noon, 33 students go home. Now there are 48 students cleaning the park. How many students helped at the start?
Show your work.

Solution ....

6 55 people are in a red train car. 29 people are in a blue train car. How many fewer people are in the blue train car than the red train car? Show your work.

Solution ....

7 First explain how to model the problem below using words. Then explain how to model it using numbers.

Kevin picks some apples. He uses 24 of the apples to make pies. He has 19 apples left. How many apples does Kevin pick?

Practice More Ways to Model Word Problems

Study the Example showing how to model with words and numbers. Then solve problems 1–6.

EXAMPLE

There are some ducks in a pond. Then 17 ducks fly away. Now there are 45 ducks in the pond. How many ducks are in the pond at the start?

Model the problem with words or with numbers. Then write an equation.

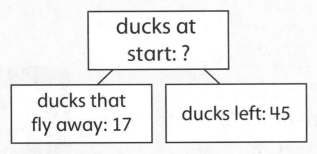

ducks at start: ?

ducks that fly away: 17

ducks left: 45

$17 + 45 = 62$

There are 62 ducks to begin with.

Rick has some grapes. Rick eats 15 of the grapes. Then he has 19 grapes left.

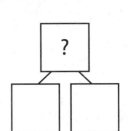

1 Complete the number bond at the right to model the problem.

2 How many grapes does Rick start with? Show your work.

Solution ....

A sports store sells baseball bats. In one week, 34 bats are sold. Then the store has 46 bats left. How many bats does the store have to begin with?

③ Model the problem with words. Complete the number bond at the right.

④ Solve the problem. Show your work.

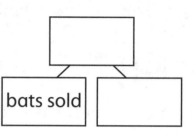

Solution ....

There are 41 people waiting at a bus stop. Then 23 of them get on a bus. Now there are 39 people on the bus.

⑤ How many people are still waiting at the bus stop now? Show your work.

Solution ....

⑥ How many people were on the bus to begin with? Show your work.

Solution ....

Develop Ways to Solve Two-Step Word Problems

Read and try to solve the problem below.

> Gabi collects 25 eggs. Her brother collects 13 eggs. Then they sell 18 eggs. How many eggs do they have now?

TRY IT

 Math Toolkit
- base-ten blocks
- number bonds
- bar models
- hundred charts
- open number lines

DISCUSS IT

Ask your partner: Do you agree with me? Why or why not?

Tell your partner: At first, I thought . . .

Explore different ways to understand how to solve two-step word problems.

> Gabi collects 25 eggs. Her brother collects 13 eggs. Then they sell 18 eggs. How many eggs do they have now?

PICTURE IT

You can draw a picture of each step.

Step 1:   25 eggs   +   13 eggs

Step 2:   38 eggs   − 18 eggs sold

MODEL IT

You can make a model of each step.

Step 1:

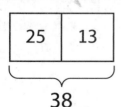

Step 2:

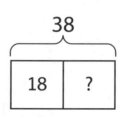

CONNECT IT

Now you will use the problem from the previous page to help you understand how to solve two-step word problems using equations.

1 Look at **Picture It**. Write an equation for Step 1.

.... + ... = ...

2 Look at **Model It**. Write an equation for Step 2.

.... − .... = ...

3 How many eggs do Gabi and her brother

have now? ....

4 How can you tell if a problem needs two steps to solve?

5 REFLECT

Look back at your **Try It**, strategies by classmates, and **Picture It** and **Model It**. Which models or strategies do you like best for solving two-step word problems? Explain.

....

....

....

APPLY IT

Use what you just learned to solve these problems.

6 Finn has 57 markers. He gives 15 markers to his brother. Then he gets 22 new markers. How many markers does Finn have now? Show your work.

Finn has .... markers now.

7 There are two bottles of juice that each hold 32 fluid ounces. Julia's family drinks 48 fluid ounces of juice. How many fluid ounces are left? Complete the bar models.

There are .... fluid ounces of juice left.

Step 1:

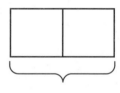

Step 2:

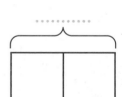

8 Anton sells 65 tickets to the play. He sells 32 on Monday and 26 on Tuesday. Choose *Yes* or *No* to tell which equations can be used in a step to find how many tickets Anton sells on Wednesday.

	Yes	No
$33 - 26 = 7$	Ⓐ	Ⓑ
$65 + 32 = 97$	Ⓒ	Ⓓ
$97 - 26 = 71$	Ⓔ	Ⓕ
$65 - 32 = 33$	Ⓖ	Ⓗ

Practice Ways to Solve Two-Step Word Problems

Study the Example showing one way to solve a two-step word problem. Then solve problems 1–4.

EXAMPLE

Mariel makes 52 fruit cups for field day. She hands out 34 fruit cups. Then she makes 15 more fruit cups. How many fruit cups does Mariel have now?

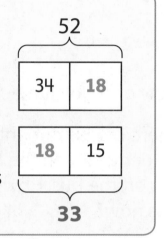

Step 1: 52 fruit cups − 34 fruit cups = **18** fruit cups

Step 2: **18** fruit cups + 15 fruit cups = **33** fruit cups

Mariel has 33 fruit cups now.

---

1 Gabe has 68 building blocks. He gets 27 more building blocks. Then he uses 73 building blocks to make a barn. How many building blocks does Gabe have left?

Show your work. Complete the bar models.

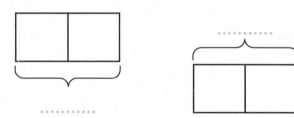

Gabe has .... building blocks left.

Lesson 9 Solve Word Problems with Two-Digit Numbers **233**

2 Amy finds 45 leaves. Nell finds 23 fewer leaves than Amy. How many leaves do they find in all?

Complete the equations for each step.

Step 1:   45 .... 23 = ...

Step 2:   45 + ... = ...

Amy and Nell have .... leaves in all.

3 There are 38 students on the bus. Then 16 more students get on the bus. At the first stop, 19 students get off the bus. How many students are on the bus now?

Complete the bar models. Show your work.

Solution ....

4 Mr. King has 75 copies of the parent letter. He gives 27 letters to Ms. Ruiz for her class to take home. Then he gives 25 letters to Mr. Allen for his class. Are there enough letters left for the 25 children in Mrs. Park's class? Explain. Show your work.

Refine Solving Word Problems with Two-Digit Numbers

Complete the Example below. Then solve problems 1–3.

EXAMPLE

Keesha's math test score is 95. John's score is 13 points less than Keesha's score. What is John's score?

You can show your work on an open number line.

Keesha's score − 13 = John's score   95 − 13 = ?

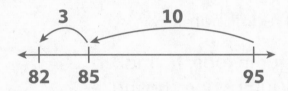

Solution ....

APPLY IT

1 There are 22 people on a train. More people get on at the next stop. Now there are 51 people on the train. How many people get on at the stop? Show your work.

> Can you make a model to help you think about the problem?

Solution ....

2 47 small dogs and 33 big dogs win a red ribbon in the pet show. 28 dogs win a blue ribbon. How many more dogs win a red ribbon than a blue ribbon? Show your work.

> How many dogs win a red ribbon?

.... more dogs win a red ribbon.

3 Liz makes 42 jumps with a jump rope. Tia makes 17 fewer jumps. How many jumps does Tia make?

> Which girl makes more jumps?

Ⓐ 24

Ⓑ 25

Ⓒ 35

Ⓓ 59

Ramin chose Ⓑ as the correct answer. How did Ramin get his answer?

Practice Solving Word Problems with Two-Digit Numbers

1 Carlos sells 32 muffins at a bake sale. Jake sells 25 fewer muffins. How many muffins does Jake sell?

Who sells more muffins?

Choose *Yes* or *No* to tell if the equation can be used to solve the problem.

	Yes	No
$25 + ? = 32$	Ⓐ	Ⓑ
$25 + 32 = ?$	Ⓒ	Ⓓ
$32 - ? = 25$	Ⓔ	Ⓕ
$32 - 25 = ?$	Ⓖ	Ⓗ

2 Some beads are in a box. Anne uses 17 of them. Then there are 56 beads in the box. How many beads are in the box to begin with?

Can you draw a model to help you think about the problem?

Ⓐ 79

Ⓑ 73

Ⓒ 39

Ⓓ 29

Dave chose Ⓒ as the correct answer. How did Dave get his answer?

3 The table shows how many roses of each color a store has for sale.

Red roses	65
Yellow roses	43
White roses	?

There are 26 fewer white roses than yellow roses. How many red and white roses does the store have in all? Show your work.

> Can you write an addition equation? Can you write a subtraction equation?

Solution ....

4 The store has 43 yellow roses. Chen buys some yellow roses. Then the store has 29 yellow roses left. How many yellow roses does Chen buy?

Ⓐ 12

Ⓑ 14

Ⓒ 36

Ⓓ 72

> What do you know? What are you trying to find out?

5 There are 23 solid shirts and 18 striped shirts on a rack. How many shirts are on the rack?

Ⓐ 5

Ⓑ 15

Ⓒ 41

Ⓓ 43

> Do you add or subtract to solve the problem?

Refine Solving Word Problems with Two-Digit Numbers

Solve the problems.

1. Ty reads 47 pages of a book. Meg reads 56 pages. How many more pages does Meg read than Ty?

   Which equations can you use to solve this problem?

   Ⓐ $56 + ? = 47$

   Ⓑ $47 + ? = 56$

   Ⓒ $56 = 47 + ?$

   Ⓓ $56 - ? = 47$

2. A beagle weighs 26 pounds. A pug weighs 8 pounds less than the beagle. How many pounds does the pug weigh?

   Ⓐ 34

   Ⓑ 20

   Ⓒ 18

   Ⓓ 13

3. Sara has 52 pens. She puts them into two cups. Complete each equation to show some of the ways Sara could put all of her pens into the two cups.

   .... + ... = 52   .... + ... = 52

   .... + ... = 52   .... + ... = 52

4 There are 64 balls and 58 bats in the gym. How many more balls are there than bats?

Can the equation be used to solve the problem?

	Yes	No
$58 + ? = 64$	Ⓐ	Ⓑ
$64 - 58 = ?$	Ⓒ	Ⓓ
$64 + 58 = ?$	Ⓔ	Ⓕ
$64 - ? = 58$	Ⓖ	Ⓗ

5 There are 100 people in line for the roller coaster. 42 people get on the roller coaster. Then 30 more people get into the line. How many people are in line now?

Ⓐ 12

Ⓑ 28

Ⓒ 72

Ⓓ 88

6 MATH JOURNAL

Write a word problem using the numbers 23 and 59. Then solve your problem.

 SELF CHECK Go back to the Unit 2 Opener and see what you can check off.

Solve Word Problems Involving Money

Dear Family,

This week your child is learning about finding the value of money and solving word problems involving coins and bills.

Your child will learn that a **penny** has a value of 1¢, a **nickel** has a value of 5¢, a **dime** has a value of 10¢, and a **quarter** has a value of 25¢.

To find the value of nickels, your child may count by fives.

5¢	5¢	5¢	5¢
5¢	10¢	15¢	20¢

The value of four nickels is 20¢.

To find the value of dimes, your child may count by tens.

10¢	10¢	10¢	10¢
10¢	20¢	30¢	40¢

The value of four dimes is 40¢.

Invite your child to share what he or she knows about money by doing the following activity together.

ACTIVITY COUNTING MONEY

Do this activity with your child to explore finding the value of money.

Materials 10 pennies (or paper circles each labeled 1¢), 10 nickels (or 10 paper circles each labeled 5¢), 10 dimes (or 10 paper circles each labeled 10¢), index cards or paper labeled 1–10

- Combine the coins and spread them out on a table. Invite your child to sort the coins and tell you the name and value of each type of coin.

- Have your child choose one type of coin. Mix the cards numbered 1–10 and let your child choose a card. Your child will make a set of coins using the number on the card. (For example, if you child chooses dimes and the number card 6, he or she will make a set of 6 dimes.)

- Encourage your child to count by ones, fives, or tens to determine the value for each set of coins. If needed, have your child place the coins in a line, and count along with your child from left to right.

- After a few rounds, ask your child to make sets of pennies, nickels, and dimes using a chosen number card. Compare the value of each set.

Explore Solving Word Problems Involving Money

You know how to solve problems with one and two-digit numbers. Use what you know to try to solve the problem below.

Lee, Seth, and Jack each have 5 coins.

Lee's coins are worth 1 cent each: ⓵¢ ⓵¢ ⓵¢ ⓵¢ ⓵¢

Seth's coins are worth 5 cents each: 5¢ 5¢ 5¢ 5¢ 5¢

Jack's coins are worth 10 cents each: 10¢ 10¢ 10¢ 10¢ 10¢

Which child has the most money?

TRY IT

 Math Toolkit
• play coins
• connecting cubes
• base-ten blocks
• hundred charts
• open number lines

 **DISCUSS IT**

Ask your partner:
Why did you choose that strategy?

Tell your partner:
At first, I thought . . .

CONNECT IT

1 LOOK BACK

Who has the most money? Explain how you know.

2 LOOK AHEAD

Use ¢ to show **cents** and $ to show **dollars**.
5¢ is 5 cents. $5 is 5 dollars.

Each type of coin and bill has a different value.

Name	Value	Front	Back
penny	1¢		
nickel	5¢		
dime	10¢		
quarter	25¢		

A $1 bill is worth the same amount as 100¢.

There are also other types of bills, such as $5, $10, $20, $50, and $100.

Fill in the blanks below.

a. .... pennies = 1 nickel

b. .... pennies = 1 dime

c. .... nickels = 1 dime

d. .... nickels = 1 quarter

3 REFLECT

Raul has 4 dimes, and Pilar has 4 nickels. Why do they have different amounts of money?

Prepare for Solving Word Problems Involving Money

1 Think about what you know about using money. Fill in each box. Use words, numbers, and pictures. Show as many ideas as you can.

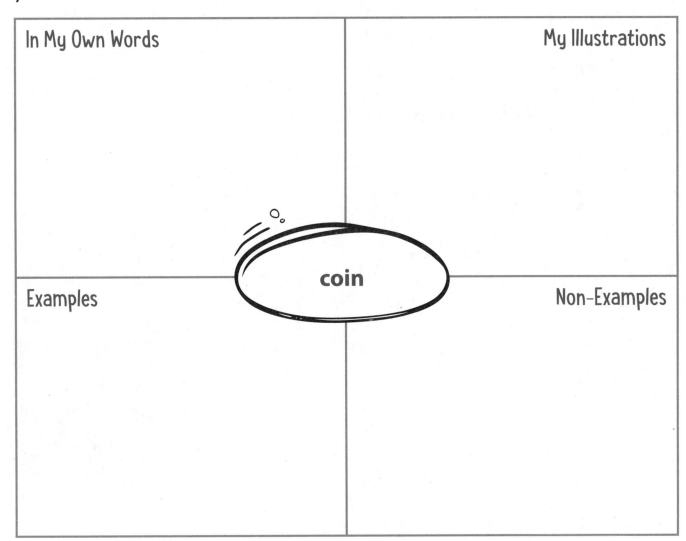

In My Own Words	My Illustrations
Examples	**Non-Examples**

coin

2 Hao has money with a total value of 10 cents. What coins could Hao have? Explain.

3 Solve the problem. Show your work.

Olga, Leti, and Jean each have 7 coins.

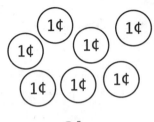

Olga

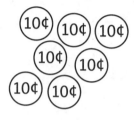

Leti

Jean

Which child has the most money?

Solution ....

4 Check your answer. Show your work.

Develop Finding the Value of Sets of Like Coins

Read and try to solve the problem below.

> **Carla needs $1 to buy a notepad. She empties her jar of nickels. Carla's nickels are shown below. Does Carla have enough money to buy a notepad?**

TRY IT

 Math Toolkit
- play coins
- connecting cubes
- base-ten blocks
- hundred charts
- open number lines

DISCUSS IT

Ask your partner:
Can you explain that again?

Tell your partner:
I started by . . .

Explore different ways to understand finding the value of groups of nickels.

> Carla needs $1 to buy a notepad. She empties her jar of nickels. Does Carla have enough money to buy a notepad?

MODEL IT
You can count by fives.

| 5 | 10 | 15 | 20 | 25 | 30 | 35 | 40 | 45 | 50 |

| 55 | 60 | 65 | 70 | 75 | 80 | 85 | 90 | 95 | 100 |

MODEL IT
You can make groups of 2 nickels. Then count by tens.

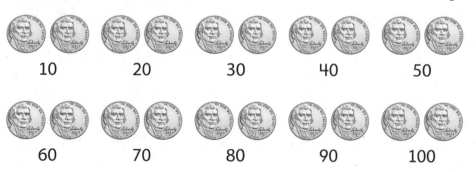

| 10 | 20 | 30 | 40 | 50 |

| 60 | 70 | 80 | 90 | 100 |

CONNECT IT

Now you will use the problem from the previous page to help you understand how to find the value of groups of nickels.

1 Look at the second **Model It**. What is the value of

2 nickels? .... ¢

2 What coin has the same value as 2 nickels? ....

3 Why can you count by tens?

4 How is counting by fives like counting by tens?

5 Does Carla have enough money to buy a notepad? How do you know?

6 REFLECT

Look back at your **Try It**, strategies by classmates, and **Model Its**. Which models or strategies do you like best for finding the value of a group of nickels? Explain.

....

....

APPLY IT

Use what you just learned to solve these problems.

7 Amy and Josh each have $1 in coins. Amy has quarters. Josh has dimes. How many of each coin do Amy and Josh have? Show your work.

Amy has .... quarters.

Josh has .... dimes.

8 Julio and Kent have the same amount of money. Julio has 1 dime. Kent has 2 coins. What coins does Kent have?

9 Sadie has the same amount of money as 1 quarter. Which group of coins could Sadie have?

Ⓐ

Ⓑ

Ⓒ

Ⓓ

Practice Finding the Value of Sets of Like Coins

Study the Example showing how to find the value of a set of coins. Then solve problems 1–5.

EXAMPLE

Danny puts these nickels in his piggy bank. How much money does Danny save?

You can make groups of 2 nickels. Then count by tens.

| 10 | 20 | 30 | 40 |

| 50 | 60 | 70 | 80 |

Danny saves 80¢.

1 Jared has these dimes. Count by tens to find the total value of the dimes. Fill in the blanks.

10¢ ....

What is the total value of Jared's coins? ....

2 Cindy has these quarters. Fill in the blanks to count the total value.

25¢ ....

How many cents does Cindy have? ....

3 What is another name for the value of

Cindy's coins? ....

4 George, Amber, and Jenna each have $1 in coins. George has quarters. Amber has dimes. Jenna has nickels. How many of each coin do George, Amber, and Jenna have? Show your work.

George has .... quarters.

Amber has .... dimes.

Jenna has .... nickels.

5 Jody has $1 in pennies. How many pennies does Jody have?

Ⓐ 4   Ⓑ 10

Ⓒ 20   Ⓓ 100

Develop Finding the Value of Sets of Mixed Coins

Read and try to solve the problem below.

> **Erik finds these coins on the floor. How many cents does he find?**

TRY IT

 Math Toolkit
- play coins
- connecting cubes
- base-ten blocks
- hundred charts
- open number lines

DISCUSS IT

Ask your partner: How did you get started?

Tell your partner: I'm not sure how to find the answer because . . .

Explore different ways to understand finding the value of coins.

> **Erik finds these coins on the floor. How many cents does he find?**

PICTURE IT

You can sort the coins and think about the value of each coin.

| 10¢ | 10¢ | 10¢ | 5¢ | 5¢ | 5¢ | 1¢ | 1¢ |

MODEL IT

You can make a model.

| 10 | 10 | 10 | 5 | 5 | 5 | 1 | 1 |

MODEL IT

You can write an addition equation.

$$10 + 10 + 10 + 5 + 5 + 5 + 1 + 1 = \,?$$

CONNECT IT

Now you will use the problem from the previous page to help you understand how to find the value of coins.

1 Look at **Picture It**. Count on by the value of each coin to find the total cents. Each time the coins change, be sure to change what you are counting by.

10¢   20¢   ....

2 Erik uses the second **Model It**. He adds values like this. Fill in the sum.

10 + 10 + 10 + 5 + 5 + 5 + 1 + 1

         30   +   15   +   2   = ...

3 Why is it helpful to sort the coins to find their total value?

4 REFLECT

Look back at your **Try It**, strategies by classmates, and **Picture It** and **Model Its**. Which models or strategies do you like best for finding the values of coins? Explain.

....

....

....

APPLY IT

Use what you just learned to solve these problems.

5 Aisha has the coins shown. How many cents does she have? Show your work.

Solution .... ¢

6 Draw another set of coins that is worth the same amount as the coins in problem 5.

7 Steve has 12¢. Then he finds these coins in his pocket. How many cents does Steve have now? Show your work.

Solution .... ¢

8 Malinda has these coins. How many cents does she have? Show your work.

Solution .... ¢

Name: _____

Practice Finding the Value of Sets of Mixed Coins

Study the Example showing how to find the value of a set of coins. Then solve problems 1–7.

EXAMPLE

Mindy has these coins. How many cents does she have?

You can count on.

25   35   45   55   60   61

Mindy has 61¢.

You can add.

25 + 10 + 10 + 10 + 5 + 1

25 + 30 + 5 + 1 = 61¢

---

1 Look at Grant's coins below. Count on to find the total value of these coins. Fill in the blanks.

10¢, _____, 25¢, _____, _____, 36¢, _____

2 Look at Grant's coins in problem 1. Add the values of the coins. Fill in the boxes.

10 + 10 + 5 + 5 + 5 + 1 + 1

☐ + 15 + ☐ = ☐ ¢

3 Look at Grant's coins in problem 1. How many cents does Grant have?

Grant has _____ ¢.

4 Hart has the coins shown at the right. How many cents does he have? Show your work.

Solution .... ¢

5 Lila has the coins shown at the right. How many cents does she have? Show your work.

Solution .... ¢

6 Ted has the coins shown at the right. How many cents does he have? Show your work.

Solution .... ¢

7 Look at the coins in problem 6. Draw a different set of coins that is worth the same amount.

Draw your coins like this:

(25) (10) (5) (1)

Develop Solving Word Problems About Money

Read and try to solve the problem below.

> Liam has a $100 bill. Kane has two $20 bills and one $5 bill. Kane gets more money for his birthday. Now he has the same amount of money as Liam. How much money does Kane get for his birthday?

TRY IT

 Math Toolkit
- play money bills
- connecting cubes
- base-ten blocks
- hundred charts
- open number lines ▸

DISCUSS IT

Ask your partner:
Do you agree with me? Why or why not?

Tell your partner:
A model I used was
... It helped me ...

Explore different ways to understand modeling word problems about money.

> Liam has a $100 bill. Kane has two $20 bills and one $5 bill. Kane gets more money for his birthday. Now he has the same amount of money as Liam. How much money does Kane get for his birthday?

MODEL IT

You can use bar models.

Step 1: Kane has two $20 bills and one $5 bill.

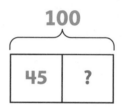

Step 2: Kane gets some more bills. Then he has $100.

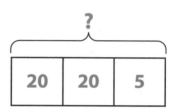

MODEL IT

You can use open number lines.

Step 1: Kane has two $20 bills and one $5 bill.

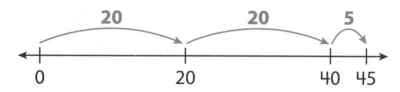

Step 2: Kane gets some more bills. Then he has $100.

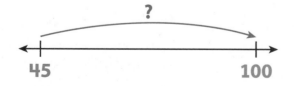

CONNECT IT

Now you will use the problem from the previous page to help you understand how to model and solve word problems about money.

1 Write an addition equation to show how much Kane starts with.

.... + ... + ... = ...

2 How much money does Kane have after his birthday? How do you know?

3 Write an equation for Step 2.

4 How much money does Kane get for his birthday? ....
Draw a set of bills that he could get.

5 REFLECT

Look back at your **Try It**, strategies by classmates, and **Model Its**. Which models or strategies do you like best for solving word problems about money? Explain.

....

....

APPLY IT

Use what you just learned to solve these problems.

6 Izzy buys a book for $13. He pays with a $20 bill. What bills could Izzy get back as change? Show your work.

Solution

7 Janet has $58 in bills in her wallet. She has one $20 bill and one $10 bill. Which other sets of bills could Janet have? Show your work.

Solution

8 Aiden is paid on Monday. On Tuesday, he is paid with a $20 bill and a $5 bill. Aiden is paid a total of $43 for both days. How much is Aiden paid on Monday?

Solution

Practice Solving Word Problems About Money

Study the Example showing how to solve a word problem about money. Then solve problems 1–7.

EXAMPLE

Kit has $50. Jan has two $10 bills and two $5 bills. Jan earns more money raking leaves. Then she has the same amount of money as Kit. How much money does Jan earn raking leaves?

Step 1: Find how much money Jan has at the start. → $10 + 10 + 5 + 5 = 30$

Step 2: Find how much money Jan earns raking leaves. → $50 - 30 = 20$

Jan earns $20 raking leaves.

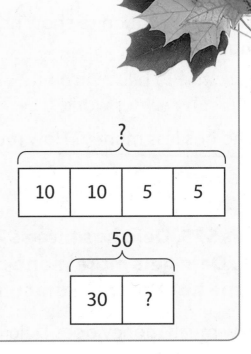

1. Show how you could use an open number line to model Step 1 of the Example. Write a number in each box.

2. Show how you could use an open number line to model Step 2 of the Example. Write a number in the box.

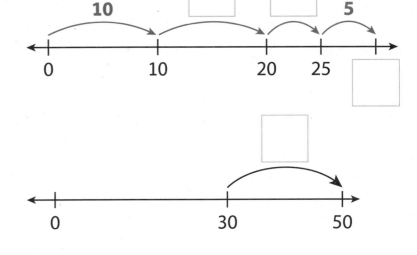

Noah has two $20 bills and one $10 bill. Thai has two $10 bills and two $5 bills.

③ Complete the equation to show how much money Noah has.

20 + 20 + 10 = ...

④ Write an equation to show how much money Thai has.

.... + ... + ... + ... = ...

⑤ Who has less money? How much less?

Ivy has $75. Deja has three $20 bills and one $5 bill. Deja gets more money recycling cans. Then she has the same amount of money as Ivy.

⑥ How much money does Deja get recycling cans? Show your work.

Solution

⑦ Ivy has 6 bills. What bills could Ivy have?

Refine Solving Word Problems Involving Money

Complete the Example below. Then solve problem 1–3.

EXAMPLE

Paige has two quarters, one dime, and one nickel. Andre has sixty cents. Who has more money? How much more?

You could add up the coins.

Paige:

$$25 + 25 + 10 + 5 = 65$$

Andre: 60 cents

$$65 - 60 = 5$$

Solution ....

APPLY IT

1 Anthony has $25 in bills. Name two ways he could have $25. Show your work.

Think about ways you could use $1, $5, $10, and $20 bills to add up to $25.

Solution ....

....

2 A pen costs 35¢. Logan pays with two quarters. What coins could Logan get back as change? Show your work.

What are two quarters worth? How do you figure out the change Logan should get?

Solution ....

3 Johanna has these coins in her pocket.

Try counting by fives to find the total.

How much are the coins worth?

Ⓐ 8¢

Ⓑ 40¢

Ⓒ 80¢

Ⓓ $2

Mary chose Ⓒ as the correct answer. How did Mary get her answer?

Practice Solving Word Problems Involving Money

1 Tell if each statement is *True* or *False*.

	True	False
One $10 bill is worth the same as two $5 bills.	Ⓐ	Ⓑ
One $20 bill is worth the same as two $10 bills.	Ⓒ	Ⓓ
Three $5 bills are worth the same as two $10 bills.	Ⓔ	Ⓕ
Four $5 bills are worth the same as two $10 bills.	Ⓖ	Ⓗ

> Can you count by 5 or 10 to help you think about each statement?

2 Dave has $45. Mac has three $5 bills and two $10 bills. Who has more money? How much more? Show your work.

> How can you find the total value of Mac's bills?

Solution ....

3 What is the total value of these coins?

> You can first find the value of each type of coin to help you solve.

Solution .... ¢

4 A pencil costs 39¢. Zack uses two quarters to pay for it. Which groups of coins could he get back in change?

What should Zack's change be worth?

Ⓐ

Ⓑ

Ⓒ

Ⓓ

5 Marcy has 27¢. Which could be Marcy's coins?

You can touch each coin as you count it to help you keep track.

Ⓐ

Ⓑ

Ⓒ

Ⓓ

Leah chose Ⓒ as the correct answer. How did Leah get her answer?

APPLY IT

Solve the problems.

1 A bookmark costs 68¢. Haley uses 3 quarters to pay for it. Which coins should she get back in change?

Ⓐ

Ⓑ

Ⓒ

Ⓓ

2 Tell if each statement is *True* or *False*.

	True	False
A dime is worth the same as ten pennies.	Ⓐ	Ⓑ
A nickel is worth the same as two dimes.	Ⓒ	Ⓓ
A quarter is worth the same as five nickels.	Ⓔ	Ⓕ
A quarter is worth the same as two dimes and one nickel.	Ⓖ	Ⓗ

3 Which sets of coins are worth 31¢?

Ⓐ

Ⓑ

Ⓒ

Ⓓ

4 Tess has more than three bills with a total value of $30. What bills could Tess have? Show your work.

Solution ....

5 Xavier answers problem 4. He says Tess could have four $10 bills. Do you agree? Explain why or why not.

6 MATH JOURNAL

Maria has $1. She spends 47¢. How much does she have left? Use pictures, words, or numbers to show your thinking.

☑ SELF CHECK Go back to the Unit 2 Opener and see what you can check off.

Tell and Write Time

Dear Family,

This week your child is learning to tell time to the nearest five minutes.

For example, he or she is learning to tell what time this clock shows.

The short hand tells the hour. It's called the hour hand. It's pointing between the 5 and the 6. The hour is 5.

The long hand shows the minutes. It's called the minute hand. It's pointing to 7. **Skip-count** by five 7 times to find how many minutes after five o'clock it is.

5, 10, 15, 20, 25, 30, 35

The time on the clock is 5:35, which is read as "five thirty-five." You can also say it is 35 minutes after five o'clock.

Digital clocks show time using only numbers instead of hands. A digital clock often shows if the time is AM or PM.

Invite your child to share what he or she knows about telling time by doing the following activity together.

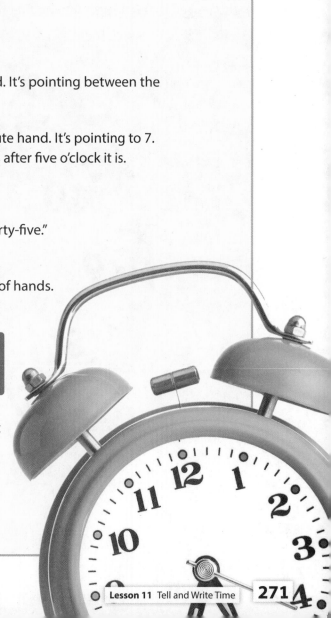

ACTIVITY TELLING TIME

Do this activity with your child to explore telling time.

Materials two crayons of different lengths

Help your child learn to show time on a clock face with this activity.

- Have family members take turns naming their favorite time of day, such as breakfast, bed time, or arriving home.

- Ask your child to place the crayons as the hands on the clock below to show the time of day that each activity happens. Help by naming the times, for example, "I get home from work at 5:20 PM" or "We eat dinner at 6:30 PM."

- Next, place the hands on the clock to show other times. Then ask your child to tell the time and describe something that happens at that time.

Explore Telling and Writing Time

You know how to tell time to the hour and half hour. Use what you know to try to solve the problem below.

> **In the afternoon Lucy starts her piano lesson at the time shown on the clock.**
>
> **What time does the clock show? Explain how you know.**

TRY IT

 Math Toolkit
- play clock with hands
- paper clock face

DISCUSS IT

Ask your partner: How did you get started?

Tell your partner: At first, I thought . . .

CONNECT IT

1 LOOK BACK

What time does Lucy start her piano lesson? ......:...... AM **or** PM

2 LOOK AHEAD

The short hand on the clock is called the hour hand.

The long hand is called the minute hand.

It takes 1 hour for the **hour hand** to move from one number to the next.

It takes 5 minutes for the **minute hand** to move from one number to the next.

AM (or a.m.) means "during the morning" and PM (or p.m.) means "noon until midnight."

a. What number did the hour hand just go past? ......

b. What number is the minute hand pointing to? ......

c. Skip-count by fives to find the number of minutes.

   5, 10, ..., ..., ..., ...

3 REFLECT

Why can you skip-count by fives to show there are 60 minutes in an hour?

....

....

....

Prepare for Telling and Writing Time

1 Think about what you know about telling time. Fill in each box. Use words, numbers, and pictures. Show as many ideas as you can.

Word	In My Own Words	Example
hour		
minute		
hour hand		
minute hand		
AM		
PM		

2 Silvia says that at 3:45, the minute hand on a clock will be pointing to the 9. Is she right? Explain.

3 Solve the problem. Show your work.

Daren starts his violin lesson at the time shown on the clock. What time does the clock show? Explain how you know.

Solution ....

4 Check your answer. Show your work.

Develop Telling and Writing Time

Read and try to solve the problem below.

> Evan starts eating breakfast at the time shown on the clock.
>
> What time does he start eating breakfast?

TRY IT

 Math Toolkit
- play clock with hands
- paper clock face

DISCUSS IT

Ask your partner:
Why did you choose that strategy?

Tell your partner:
I knew . . . so I . . .

Explore different ways to understand telling and writing time.

> **Evan starts eating breakfast at the time shown on the clock.**
>
> **What time does he start eating breakfast?**

PICTURE IT

You can use the clock to find the hour and minutes.

The hour hand is between the **7** and the **8**.

The minute hand is pointed at the **4**.

Skip-count by five **4** times to find the minutes.

PICTURE IT

You can use a time you already know to find the hour and minutes.

The clock shows **7:15**, which is read as "seven fifteen."

You can add **5 more** to find the minutes.

$$15 + 5 = ?$$

CONNECT IT

Now you will use the problem from the previous page to help you understand how to tell and write time.

1 What time does Evan start eating breakfast? .... : .... AM or PM

2 The clock shows the time Evan finishes breakfast. Tell how you know what the hour is.

3 How can you skip-count to find the number of minutes on the clock when Evan finishes breakfast?

4 What time does Evan finish breakfast? Show the time on the digital clock. Circle AM or PM.

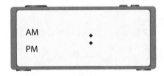

5 REFLECT

Look back at your **Try It**, strategies by classmates, and **Picture Its**. Which models or strategies do you like best for telling and writing time? Explain.

....

....

APPLY IT

Use what you just learned to solve these problems.

6 The top clock shows when Mark goes to bed. Write the same time on the digital clock. What time does Mark go to bed? Circle AM or PM. Show your work.

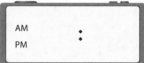

Solution ....

7 Kate gets home from school at the time shown on the clock. Circle AM or PM.

Show the same time by drawing the hands on this clock.

8 Sasha eats lunch at 11:40 AM. Which clock shows the time she eats lunch?

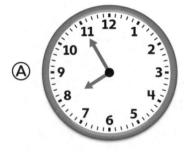

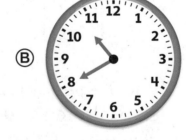

Practice Telling and Writing Time

Study the Example showing how to tell and write time. Then solve problems 1–6.

EXAMPLE

The top clock shows when Lil starts eating dinner. Show the same time on a digital clock.

The hour hand is just past the 6, so the hour is 6.

The minute hand points to the 4. So, skip-count by five 4 times to find the number of minutes.

5, 10, 15, 20

The time is 6:20 PM. Read the time by saying "six twenty."

PM **6:20**

1 Gino goes on a picnic in the afternoon. The first clock shows when the picnic starts. Show how the time would look on a digital clock. Circle AM or PM.

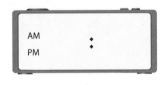

AM
PM

2 Nima's soccer team plays on Sunday mornings. Her first game starts at the time shown on the digital clock. Draw the same time on the other clock.

AM **9:45**

3 Bryce has a piano lesson after school. His lesson ends at the time shown on the digital clock. Draw the same time on the other clock.

4 The first clock shows when Nadya brushes her teeth before school. Show how the time would look on a digital clock. Circle AM or PM.

5 The first clock shows when Mr. Wade's class starts recess. Show how the time would look on a digital clock. Circle AM or PM.

6 Eric calls his aunt at 10:15 in the morning. Draw hands on the clock to show 10:15. Then write the time on the digital clock. Circle AM or PM.

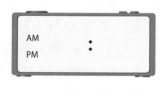

Refine Telling and Writing Time

Complete the Example below. Then solve problems 1–3.

EXAMPLE

In the afternoon Dina goes on a bike ride at the time shown on the clock. What time does the clock show?

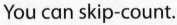

You can skip-count.
The hour hand is past the 2
but not to the 3 yet. So, the hour is 2.
The minute hand is on the 9, so skip-count by five 9 times to find the number of minutes.

    5, 10, 15, 20, 25, 30, 35, 40, 45

Solution ....

APPLY IT

1 Caleb plays basketball on Saturday mornings. His game starts at the time shown on the clock.

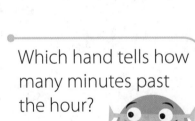

Which hand tells how many minutes past the hour?

Show the same time on the digital clock.
Circle AM or PM.

2 Sophia has a meeting at the time shown on the digital clock below. Show the same time on the other clock.

What two numbers will the hour hand be between? What number will the minute hand point to?

3 Jane gets home from school at the time shown on the clock. What time does Jane get home?

Ⓐ 5:15

Ⓑ 3:05

Ⓒ 3:25

Ⓓ 4:25

Which hand tells the hour?

Emily chose Ⓑ as the correct answer. How did Emily get her answer?

Practice Telling and Writing Time

1   Luis gets home from school at 3:25. Which clocks show the time Luis gets home?

What two numbers will the hour hand be between?

Ⓐ

Ⓑ PM **3:25**

Ⓒ

Ⓓ

Ⓔ

2   Justin finishes art class at 2:40 in the afternoon. Draw hands on the clock to show 2:40. Then write the time on the digital clock. Circle AM or PM.

Is the hour hand or minute hand longer?

AM
PM   :

3   Which number does the minute hand point to when a clock shows 5:10?

Can you draw a picture to help you?

Ⓐ 10   Ⓑ 5

Ⓒ 3   Ⓓ 2

4 Lita's mom wakes her up to get ready for school at the time shown on the clock. Which digital clock shows the time Lita's mom wakes her up?

Where does the hour hand point when it is almost the next hour?

Ⓐ  PM 11:35

Ⓑ  AM 6:55

Ⓒ  AM 7:55

Ⓓ  PM 7:11

5 Rory has dance class on Saturdays at the time shown on the clock. What time does Rory have dance class?

Which hand tells the minutes?

Ⓐ 3:09   Ⓑ 3:45

Ⓒ 9:15   Ⓓ 9:30

Mike chose Ⓑ as the correct answer. How did Mike get his answer?

Refine Telling and Writing Time

APPLY IT
Solve the problems.

1 Elsa goes to swim practice after school. She finishes at 5:45. Which clocks show the time Elsa finishes?

Ⓐ AM **4:55**

Ⓑ

Ⓒ

Ⓓ PM **5:45**

Ⓔ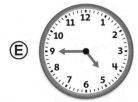

2 Where does the hour hand point when a clock shows 10:30?

Ⓐ at the 6　　　　Ⓑ between the 9 and the 10

Ⓒ at the 10　　　Ⓓ between the 10 and the 11

3 The minute hand on a clock points at the 10. What time could it be?

Ⓐ 10:10　　　　Ⓑ 4:50

Ⓒ 10:30　　　　Ⓓ 8:50

Ⓔ 10:20

4 Dylan finishes soccer practice at the time shown on the clock at the right.

Which clock below shows the time Dylan finishes soccer practice?

AM 4:01 PM 4:05 AM 1:20 PM 4:10

Ⓐ Ⓑ Ⓒ Ⓓ

5 After school Robin reads until 7:35. Draw hands on the clock to show that time. Then write the same time on the digital clock. Circle AM or PM.

AM
PM

6 When Jane gets home, the hour hand is just past the 6, and the minute hand is pointing to the 5. What time does Jane get home? You can use the clock picture to help you answer.

7 MATH JOURNAL

The clock at the right is missing the minute hand. It is either 6:05 or 6:55. Which is correct? Explain how the hour hand can help you know the answer.

☑ SELF CHECK Go back to the Unit 2 Opener and see what you can check off.

In this unit you learned to . . .

Skill	Lesson
Add two-digit numbers.	6, 8
Add tens and add ones.	6, 7, 8
Regroup ones as a ten and decompose a ten.	6, 7
Subtract two-digit numbers.	7, 8
Solve one-step and two-step word problems by adding or subtracting two-digit numbers.	9
Solve word problems involving money.	10
Tell and write time to the nearest 5 minutes.	11

Think about what you learned.

Use words, numbers, and drawings.

1 One topic I could use in my everyday life is .... because . . .

2 I would like to learn more about how to . . .

3 One thing I could do better is . . .

Work with Two-Digit Numbers, Time, and Money

Study an Example Problem and Solution

SMP 1 Make sense of problems and persevere in solving them.

Zoo Tours

A total of 58 people sign up for a tour of the zoo today. Alex has to make groups for the tour. Look at the notes.

Zoo Tour Notes

- Tour groups must have at least 12 people.
- Tour groups can have no more than 20 people.
- There can be up to 4 tour groups in one day.

Help Alex decide how to put the 58 people into tour groups.

Show how Yoop's solution matches the checklist.

☑ PROBLEM-SOLVING CHECKLIST

☐ Tell what is known.
☐ Tell what the problem is asking.
☐ Show all your work.
☐ Show that the solution works.

a. Circle something that is known.

b. Underline something that you need to find.

c. Draw a box around what you do to solve the problem.

d. Put a checkmark next to the part that shows that the solution works.

YOOP'S SOLUTION

- **I know** there are 58 people to put into groups. I can make up to 4 groups with between 12 and 20 people.

- **I need to find** the number of groups to make and how many people are in each group.

- **I can start** with the least number, which is 12 in a group.

  4 groups: $12 + 12 + 12 + 12 = 48$

- **I can subtract** 48 from the total number of people.

  $58 - 48 = 10$

- **Now I can find** four numbers that add to 10.

  $3 + 3 + 2 + 2 = 10$

  Add 3 people to two groups and add 2 people to two groups.

  $12 + 3 = 15$

  $12 + 2 = 14$

- **Make these groups:**

  15 people

  15 people

  14 people

  14 people

- **Add to check:**

  $15 + 15 + 14 = 44$

  $44 + 14 = 58$

Hi, I'm Yoop. Here's how I solved this problem.

I decided to make 4 groups so the groups will have fewer people.

So there are 10 people that still have to be put into a group.

Try Another Approach

There are many ways to solve problems. Think about how you might solve the Zoo Tours problem in a different way.

Zoo Tours

A total of 58 people sign up for a tour of the zoo today. Alex has to make groups for the tour. Look at the notes.

Zoo Tour Notes

- Tour groups must have at least 12 people.
- Tour groups can have no more than 20 people.
- There can be up to 4 tour groups in one day.

Help Alex decide how to put the 58 people into tour groups.

PLAN IT

Answer this question to help you start thinking about a plan.

What could you do if you want to make larger groups of people? Explain your thinking.

SOLVE IT

**Find a different solution for the Zoo Tours problem.
Show all your work on a separate sheet of paper.**

You may want to use the Problem-Solving Tips to get started.

PROBLEM-SOLVING TIPS

- **Questions**
  - What are the different numbers I can use for the people in a tour group?
  - What is the fewest number of groups I can use?

- **Word Bank**

add	most	total
subtract	least	difference

- **Sentence Starters**
  - I can use _____
  - The most people _____
  - The total number _____

☑ **PROBLEM-SOLVING CHECKLIST**

Make sure that you . . .
- ☐ tell what you know.
- ☐ tell what you need to do.
- ☐ show all your work.
- ☐ show that the solution works.

REFLECT

Use Mathematical Practices Talk about this question with a partner.

- **Show and Explain** Why does your solution work? Explain to your partner.

Discuss Models and Strategies

Solve the problem on a separate sheet of paper.
There are different ways you can solve it.

Butterfly Garden

Alex is making a butterfly garden. She is trying to decide what flower seeds to buy. Here are her notes.

Butterfly Garden Notes
- Buy 3 or 4 pounds of seeds.
- Spend up to $100 on seeds.

Here are the seeds she can choose from.
- Butterfly Mix: $25 for 1 pound
- Wildflower Mix: $28 for 1 pound
- Early Bloom Mix: $24 for 1 pound
- Late Bloom Mix: $22 for 1 pound

What seeds should Alex buy? What is the total cost?
If there is money left over, tell how much.

PLAN IT AND SOLVE IT

Find a solution to the Butterfly Garden problem.

- Show what kinds of seeds and how many packets to buy.
- Find the total cost and show if there is any money left over.

You may want to use the Problem-Solving Tips to get started.

PROBLEM-SOLVING TIPS

- **Questions**
  - How many packets of seeds do I need to buy?
  - Do I want to buy a mix of different seeds?

- **Word Bank**

add	total	left over
subtract	difference	cost

- **Sentence Starters**
  - The price _____
  - I can spend _____
  - The total cost _____

☑ **PROBLEM-SOLVING CHECKLIST**

Make sure that you . . .
- ☐ tell what you know.
- ☐ tell what you need to do.
- ☐ show all your work.
- ☐ show that the solution works.

REFLECT

Use Mathematical Practices Talk about this question with a partner.

- **Make an Argument** How can you explain the reason for the seeds that you choose?

Persevere On Your Own

Solve each problem on a separate sheet of paper.

The Birdhouse Builders

The zoo gives money to the Birdhouse Builders, who make houses for endangered birds. The zoo collects money at the bird show. People at the show can hold up a $1 bill, a $5 bill, or a $10 bill. The birds fly around and collect the money.

It costs $25 to make one birdhouse. What are two different ways to make $25 with these bills?

SOLVE IT

Show two ways to make $25 with these bills.

• Tell how many of each bill to use.

• Show why your answer works.

REFLECT

Use Mathematical Practices Talk about this question with a partner.

• **Choose a Tool** What tools did you use to solve this problem?

Sea Lion Show

Alex is helping the zoo plan a new sea lion show.
Here are her notes.

- There are 3 shows each day.
- All the shows start at 10 minutes past an hour.
- One show starts in the morning.
- One show starts after 2:00 but before 2:30.
- One show starts after 2:30 but before 3:30

What time should each show start?

Show 1 Time: _____   Show 2 Time: _____   Show 3 Time: _____

SOLVE IT
Help Alex decide what time each show starts.

- Write the start times. Show the times on the clocks.

- Explain why your solution works for all items in the notes

REFLECT
Use Mathematical Practices Talk about this question
with a partner.

- **Make Sense of Problems** How did you decide the start
times for the shows?

UNIT 2

Unit Review

1. Find 56 + 27.

   Ⓐ 73

   Ⓑ 77

   Ⓒ 83

   Ⓓ 87

2. Bill and Maya are reading the same book. Yesterday, Maya read 16 more pages than Bill did. Maya read 43 pages yesterday.

   Part A

   How many pages did Bill read yesterday? Show your work.

   Bill read .... pages yesterday.

   Part B

   Today, Bill reads 38 pages. How many more pages did Bill read today than yesterday? Show your work.

   Bill read .... more pages today.

3 Joshua counts 25 goats in a herd and 18 pigs in a pen. Which equations can Joshua use to find how many more goats there are than pigs? Choose all the correct answers.

Ⓐ $25 - 18 = ?$

Ⓑ $25 + 18 = ?$

Ⓒ $? - 25 = 18$

Ⓓ $18 + ? = 25$

Ⓔ $25 - ? = 18$

4 Samantha has 67 cents. Eric has one quarter, two dimes, and three pennies. Who has more money? How much more? Show your work.

Solution ....

5 Greta gets home from practice at the time shown on the clock. What time does Greta get home from practice?

Write your answer in the blanks.

.... : ....

Performance Task

Answer the questions. Show all your work on separate paper.

Nicole bakes chocolate and vanilla cupcakes for a party.

Some of the cupcakes have frosting. The rest have no frosting.

Use the clues to find how many of each type of cupcake Nicole bakes.

- There are 34 chocolate cupcakes with frosting.
- There are 11 vanilla cupcakes with no frosting.
- There are 80 cupcakes in all.
- There are 26 fewer chocolate cupcakes with no frosting than with frosting.

	Chocolate Cupcakes	Vanilla Cupcakes	Total
Frosting			
No Frosting			
Total			

Copy and complete the table on a separate piece of paper. Explain why your answer works.

REFLECT

Model with Mathematics Tell how you can use the table to help you check your work. Then check to make sure the numbers in your table are correct.

Draw or write to show examples for each term. Then draw or write to show other math words in the unit.

AM (or a.m.) morning, or the time from midnight until before noon.

My Example

cent (¢) the smallest unit of money in the U.S. One penny has a value of 1 cent. 100 cents is equal to 1 dollar.

My Example

dime a coin with a value of 10 cents (10¢).

My Example

dollar ($) a unit of money in the U.S. There are 100 cents in 1 dollar ($1).

My Example

hundreds groups of 10 tens.

My Example

penny a coin with a value of 1 cent (1¢).

My Example

nickel   a coin with a value of 5 cents (5¢).

My Example

PM (or p.m.)   the time from noon until before midnight.

My Example

quarter   a coin with a value of 25 cents (25¢).

My Example

regroup   to put together or break apart ones, tens, or hundreds. For example, 10 ones can be regrouped as 1 ten, or 1 hundred can be regrouped as 10 tens.

My Example

skip-count   count by a number other than ones, such as count by twos, fives, tens, or hundreds.

My Example

My Word: _____

_____

_____

My Example

Set 1: Number Partners for 10

Fill in the blanks to make the equations true.

1 $7 + \underline{\hspace{2cm}} = 10$ **2** $5 + \underline{\hspace{2cm}} = 10$ **3** $\underline{\hspace{2cm}} + 2 = 10$

4 $10 - 4 = \underline{\hspace{2cm}}$ **5** $10 - \underline{\hspace{2cm}} = 3$ **6** $10 - \underline{\hspace{2cm}} = 1$

Set 2: Add and Subtract in Word Problems

Fill in the blanks to solve the problems.

1 2 cats sit on a rock. More cats come. Now there are 5 cats on the rock. How many more cats came?

$2 + \underline{\hspace{2cm}} = 5$

$\underline{\hspace{2cm}}$ more cats came.

2 Liam has some beads. His friend gives him 2 more beads. Now Liam has 9 beads. How many beads did Liam have to start?

$\underline{\hspace{2cm}} + 2 = \underline{\hspace{2cm}}$

Liam had $\underline{\hspace{1.5cm}}$ beads to start.

3 Kim has 8 crayons. She gives some away. Now she has 3 crayons. How many does she give away?

$8 - \underline{\hspace{2cm}} = 3$

Kim gives away $\underline{\hspace{1.5cm}}$ crayons.

4 There are 9 pencils. There are 3 markers. How many more pencils are there?

$9 - \underline{\hspace{2cm}} = \underline{\hspace{2cm}}$

$\underline{\hspace{2cm}}$ more pencils.

Set 3: Write True Equations

Find partners with equal totals. Complete the equations.

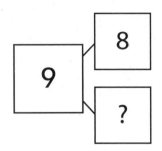

1

$9 = 8 +$ ....

$6 +$ .... $= 9$

$8 +$ .... $=$ .... $+$ ....

Set 4: Make a Ten to Add or Subtract

Make a ten to solve the problems.

1 $9 + 3 = ?$

9 $+$ 3

$10 +$ .... $=$ ....

$9 + 3 =$ ....

2 $8 + 7 = ?$

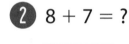

8 $+$ 7

$10 +$ .... $=$ ....

$8 + 7 =$ ....

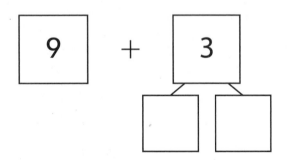

3 $13 - 6 = ?$

$6 +$ .... $= 10$

$10 +$ .... $= 13$

$6 +$ .... $= 13$

So, $13 - 6 =$ ....

4 $15 - 9 = ?$

$9 +$ .... $= 10$

$10 +$ .... $= 15$

$9 +$ .... $= 15$

So, $15 - 9 =$ ....

5 $17 - 8 = ?$

$8 +$ .... $= 10$

$10 +$ .... $= 17$

$8 +$ .... $= 17$

So, $17 - 8 =$ ....

Set 5: Add Three Numbers

Fill in the blanks to solve the problems.

1 7 people are at a party. 4 more people come. Then 7 more people come.

How many people are at the party now?

.... + ... + ... = ... people

2 Emma has 4 blue beads, 2 red beads, and 8 green beads.

How many beads does Emma have?

.... + ... + ... = ... beads

3 Find $5 + 5 + 8$.

.... + ... $= 10$

$10 +$ .... $=$ .... $5 + 5 + 8 =$ ....

Set 6: Find the Unknown Number

Find the missing numbers.

1 .... $+ 3 = 11$ **2** $9 +$ .... $= 13$ **3** $7 + 5 =$ ....

4 $15 - 8 =$ ....   **5** .... $- 6 = 8$ **6** $16 - 7 =$ ....

Set 7: Compare Numbers

Write <, >, or = in the circle.

1 72 ◯ 72   **2** 50 ◯ 54   **3** 61 ◯ 64

4 39 ◯ 45   **5** 29 ◯ 28   **6** 65 ◯ 55

Set 8: Add and Subtract Tens

Fill in the blanks.

1 Find 20 + 70.

.... tens + ... tens = ... tens

20 + 70 = ...

2 Find 40 + ? = 60.

.... tens + ... tens = ... tens

40 + ... = 60

3 Find 80 − 30.

.... tens − .... tens = ... tens

80 − 30 = ...

4 10 less than 88 is ....

5 10 more than 32 is ....

6 10 more than 45 is ....

7 10 less than 24 is ....

Set 9: Compare Length

Fill in the blanks.

1
The .... ribbon is longest.

The .... ribbon is shortest.

2 Tina is taller than Jamal. Zach is shorter than Jamal.

Tina is .... than Zach.

Zach is .... than Tina.

Cumulative Practice

Name: _____

Set 1: Count On to Add

What number do you get after you count on:

1 1 more than 7? ....

2 3 more than 6? ....

3 3 more than 2? ....

4 2 more than 7? ....

5 2 more than 9? ....

6 3 more than 9? ....

Set 2: Two-Step Word Problems

Solve the word problems. Show your work.

1 There are 16 people on a bus. At the first stop, 9 people get off the bus and 4 people get on. How many people are on the bus now?

2 Denise puts 6 blue marbles and 7 red marbles in a bag. Then she adds some yellow marbles. Now, there are 16 marbles in the bag. How many yellow marbles does Denise put in the bag?

3 Ricky fills 12 balloons with helium. Then 4 of the balloons pop and 5 float away. How many balloons does Ricky have left?

Set 3: Use Addition to Subtract

Fill in the blanks in each equation.

1 $15 - 9 = ?$ is the same as .... $+ ? =$ ....

2 $12 - 8 = ?$ is the same as .... $+ ? =$ ....

3 $13 - 9 = ?$ is the same as .... $+ ? =$ ....

Set 4: Make a Ten to Subtract

Fill in the squares.

1 Make a ten to find $17 - 9$.

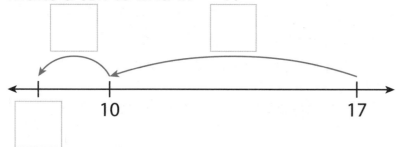

$17 - 9 =$ ☐

2 Make a ten to find $14 - 8$.

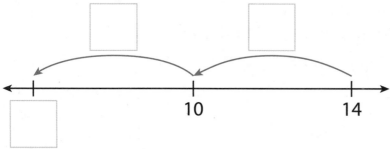

$14 - 8 =$ ☐

3 Make a ten to find $11 - 7$.

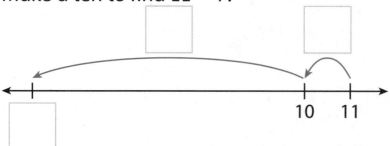

$11 - 7 =$ ☐

Set 5: One-Step Word Problems

Solve the word problems. Show your work with an equation.

1 Leon has 14 trading cards. He gives some to his cousin. Now Leon has 8 trading cards left. How many trading cards does Leon give to his cousin?

2 Mrs. Murphy has some chickens. Her son brought her 5 more chickens. Now she has 12 chickens. How many chickens did Mrs. Murphy have to begin with?

Set 6: Fact Families

Complete the number bond and write equations for the fact family.

1 16 / 9 7

.... + ... = 16   16 − .... = ...

.... + ... = 16   16 − .... = ...

2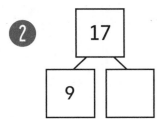

.... + ... = 17   17 − .... = ...

.... + ... = 17   17 − .... = ...

3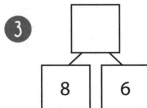

.... + ... = ... − .... = ...

.... + ... = ... − .... = ...

Set 7: Doubles and Doubles Plus 1

Solve the problems.

1 $7 + 7 =$ ....

2 $9 + 9 =$ ....

3 $6 + 6 =$ ....

4 $5 + 6 =$ ....

5 $7 + 8 =$ ....

6 $8 + 9 =$ ....

Set 8: Make a Ten to Add

Fill in the squares and the blanks.

1 Make a ten to find $7 + 8$.

$7 +$　　　$8 = ?$

$7 +$ ☐ $+$ ☐

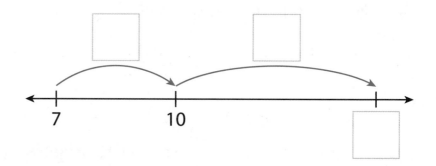

So, $7 + 8 =$ ....

2 Make a ten to find $5 + 9$.

$5 +$　　　$9 = ?$

$5 +$ ☐ $+$ ☐

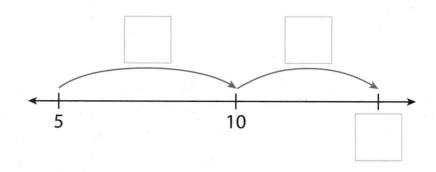

So, $5 + 9 =$ ....

3 Make a ten to find $6 + 7$.

$6 +$　　　$7 = ?$

$6 +$ ☐ $+$ ☐

So, $6 + 7 =$ ....

Glossary/Glosario

English	Español	Example/Ejemplo

Aa

add
to put together two or more quantities, to find the total of two or more numbers, or to find how many in all.

sumar
combinar dos o más cantidades, hallar el total de dos o más números, o hallar cuántos hay en total.

$27 + 15 = 42$

---

addend
a number being added.

sumando
número que se suma.

$4 + 7 = 11$

addends

AM (or a.m.)
morning, or the time from midnight until before noon.

a. m.
el tiempo que transcurre desde la medianoche hasta el mediodía.

AM 7:20

---

analog clock
a clock that uses hour and minute hand positions to show time.

reloj analógico
reloj que muestra la hora con una manecilla de la hora y un minutero.

hour hand — minute hand

---

angle
one of the corners of a shape where two sides meet.

ángulo
una de las esquinas de una figura en la que se unen dos lados.

angle

---

array
a set of objects arranged in equal rows and equal columns.

matriz
conjunto de objetos agrupados en filas y columnas iguales.

☆ ☆ ☆ ☆ ☆
☆ ☆ ☆ ☆ ☆
☆ ☆ ☆ ☆ ☆

English	Español	Example/Ejemplo
associative property of addition when the grouping of three or more addends is changed, the total does not change.	**propiedad asociativa de la suma** cambiar la agrupación de tres o más sumandos no cambia el total.	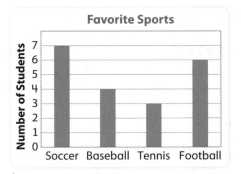$(2 + 3) + 4 = 2 + (3 + 4)$

Bb

bar graph a data display in which bars are used to show the number of items in each category.	**gráfica de barras** representación de datos en la cual se usan barras para mostrar el número de elementos de cada categoría.	

Cc

cent (¢) the smallest unit of money in the U.S. One penny has a value of 1 cent. 100 cents is equal to 1 dollar.	**centavo (¢)** la menor unidad monetaria de Estados Unidos. 100 centavos equivalen a 1 dólar.	 1 cent 1¢
centimeter (cm) a unit of length. There are 100 centimeters in 1 meter.	**centímetro (cm)** unidad de longitud. 100 centímetros equivalen a 1 metro.	Your little finger is about 1 **centimeter** (cm) across.

English	Español	Example/Ejemplo
column a top-to-bottom (vertical) line of objects or numbers, such as in an array or table.	**columna** línea de objetos o números vertical (que va de arriba abajo), como las de una matriz o una tabla.	
commutative property of addition changing the order of addends does not change the total.	**propiedad conmutativa de la suma** cambiar el orden de los sumandos no cambia el total.	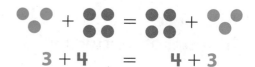 3 + 4 = 4 + 3
compare to decide if numbers, amounts, or sizes are greater than, less than, or equal to each other.	**comparar** determinar si un número, una cantidad o un tamaño es mayor que, menor que o igual a otro número, otra cantidad u otro tamaño.	421 > 312
count on start with one addend and count to find a total.	**contar hacia delante** comenzar desde un sumando y contar para hallar un total.	8 + 3 = ? 8, then 9, 10, 11 8 + 3 = 11
cube a solid shape with 6 square faces and all sides of equal length.	**cubo** figura sólida que tiene 6 caras cuadradas y todos los lados de igual longitud.	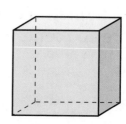

English	Español	Example/Ejemplo

Dd

data
a set of collected information.

datos
conjunto de información reunida.

Favorite Toys

---

difference
the result of subtraction.

diferencia
el resultado de la resta.

$9 - 3 = 6$

---

digit
a symbol used to write numbers.

dígito
símbolo que se usa para escribir números.

The digits are 0, 1, 2, 3, 4, 5, 6, 7, 8, and 9.

---

digital clock
a clock that uses digits to show the time.

reloj digital
reloj que usa dígitos para mostrar la hora.

---

dime
a coin with a value of 10 cents (10¢).

moneda de 10¢
moneda con un valor de 10 centavos (10¢).

10 cents   10¢

---

dollar ($)
a unit of money in the U.S. There are 100 cents in 1 dollar ($1).

dólar
unidad monetaria de Estados Unidos. 1 dólar ($1) equivale a 100 centavos.

English	Español	Example/Ejemplo

Ee

edge
a line segment where two faces meet in a three-dimensional shape.

arista
segmento de recta donde se encuentran dos caras de una figura tridimensional.

Edge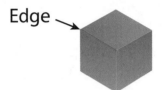

---

equal
having the same value, same size, or same amount.

igual
que tiene el mismo valor, el mismo tamaño, o la misma cantidad.

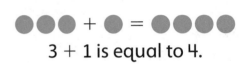
3 + 1 is equal to 4.

---

equal sign (=)
a symbol that means *is the same value as*.

signo de igual (=)
símbolo que significa *tiene el mismo valor que*.

$12 + 4 = 16$

---

equation
a mathematical statement that uses an equal sign (=) to show that two things have the same value.

ecuación
enunciado matemático en el que se usa un signo de igual (=) para mostrar que dos cosas tienen el mismo valor.

$25 - 15 = 10$

---

estimate (noun)
a close guess made using mathematical thinking.

estimación
suposición aproximada que se hace usando el razonamiento matemático.

$28 + 21 = ?$
$30 + 20 = 50$
50 is an estimate of the sum.

---

estimate (verb)
to make a close guess based on mathematical thinking.

estimar / hacer una estimación
hacer una suposición aproximada usando el razonamiento matemático.

28 + 21 is about 50.

English	Español	Example/Ejemplo
even number a whole number that always has 0, 2, 4, 6, or 8 in the ones place. An even number of objects can be put into pairs or into two equal groups without any leftovers.	**número par** número entero que siempre tiene 0, 2, 4, 6, o 8 en la posición de las unidades. Un número par de objetos puede agruparse en parejas o en dos grupos iguales sin sobrantes.	20, 22, 24, 26, and 28 are even numbers.
expanded form a way a number is written to show the place value of each digit.	**forma desarrollada** manera de escribir un número para mostrar el valor posicional de cada dígito.	$249 = 200 + 40 + 9$

Ff

English	Español	Example/Ejemplo
face a flat surface of a solid shape.	**cara** superficie plana de una figura sólida.	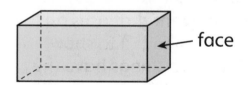 face
fact family a group of related equations that use the same numbers, but in a different order and two different operation symbols. A fact family can show the relationship between addition and subtraction.	**familia de datos** grupo de ecuaciones relacionadas que tienen los mismos números ordenados de distinta manera y dos símbolos de operaciones diferentes. Una familia de datos puede mostrar la relación que existe entre la suma y la resta.	$7 - 3 = 4$ $7 - 4 = 3$ $3 + 4 = 7$ $4 + 3 = 7$

English	Español	Example/Ejemplo
foot (ft) a unit of length. There are 12 inches in 1 foot.	**pie (ft)** unidad de longitud. 1 pie equivale a 12 pulgadas.	12 inches = 1 foot
fourths the parts formed when a whole is divided into four equal parts.	**cuartos** partes que se forman cuando se divide un entero en cuatro partes iguales.	fourths 4 equal parts

Gg

English	Español	Example/Ejemplo
greater than symbol (>) a symbol used to compare two numbers when the first is greater than the second.	**símbolo de mayor que (>)** símbolo que se usa para comparar dos números cuando el primero es mayor que el segundo.	421 > 312

Hh

English	Español	Example/Ejemplo
halves the parts formed when a whole is divided into two equal parts.	**medios** partes que se obtienen cuando se divide un entero en dos partes iguales.	2 equal parts
hexagon a two-dimensional closed shape with 6 straight sides and 6 angles.	**hexágono** figura bidimensional cerrada que tiene 6 lados y 6 ángulos.	
hour (h) a unit of time. There are 60 minutes in 1 hour.	**hora (h)** unidad de tiempo. 1 hora equivale a 60 minutos.	60 minutes = 1 hour

English	Español	Example/Ejemplo
hour hand the shorter hand on a clock. It shows the hours.	**manecilla de la hora** la manecilla más corta de un reloj. Muestra las horas.	 hour hand
hundreds groups of 10 tens.	**centenas** grupos de 10 decenas.	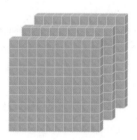

Ii

English	Español	Example/Ejemplo
inch (in.) a unit of length. There are 12 inches in 1 foot.	**pulgada (pulg.)** unidad de longitud del sistema usual. 12 pulgadas equivalen a 1 pie.	A quarter is about 1 **inch** (in.) across. 

Ll

English	Español	Example/Ejemplo
length measurement that tells the distance from one point to another, or how long something is.	**longitud** medida que indica la distancia de un punto a otro, o cuán largo es un objeto.	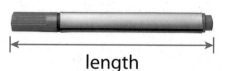 length

English	Español	Example/Ejemplo
less than symbol (<) a symbol used to compare two numbers when the first is less than the second.	**símbolo de menor que (<)** símbolo que se usa para comparar dos números cuando el primero es menor que el segundo.	$321 < 421$
line plot a data display that shows data as marks above a number line.	**diagrama de puntos** representación de datos en la cual se muestran datos como marcas sobre una recta numérica.	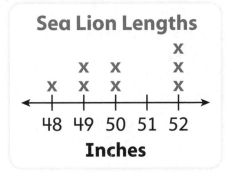
longer having a length that is greater than that of another object.	**más largo** que tiene una longitud mayor que la de otro objeto.	

Mm

English	Español	Example/Ejemplo
measure to find length, height, or weight by comparing it to a known unit.	**medir** determinar la longitud, la altura o el peso de un objeto comparándolo con una unidad conocida.	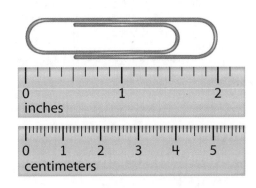

English	Español	Example/Ejemplo
measuring tape a flexible measuring strip that shows inches and centimeters.	**cinta de medir** una tira flexible que se usa para medir y muestra pulgadas y centímetros.	
meter (m) a unit of length. There are 100 centimeters in 1 meter.	**metro (m)** unidad de longitud. 1 metro es igual a 100 centímetros.	100 centimeters = 1 meter
meter stick a measuring stick that is 1 meter long and shows 100 centimeters.	**metro** una regla que mide 1 metro de longitud y muestra 100 centímetros.	
minute (min) a unit of time. There are 60 minutes in 1 hour.	**minuto (min)** unidad de tiempo. 60 minutos equivalen a 1 hora.	60 minutes = 1 hour
minute hand the longer hand on a clock. It shows minutes.	**minutero** la manecilla más larga de un reloj. Muestra los minutos.	minute hand 

Nn

nickel a coin with a value of 5 cents (5¢).	**moneda de 5¢** moneda con un valor de 5 centavos (5¢).	 5 cents 5¢

English	Español	Example/Ejemplo
number line a straight line marked at equal spaces to show numbers.	**recta numérica** recta que tiene marcas separadas por espacios iguales; las marcas muestran números.	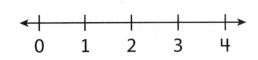

Oo

English	Español	Example/Ejemplo
odd number a whole number that always has 1, 3, 5, 7, or 9 in the ones place. An odd number of objects cannot be put into pairs or into two equal groups without a leftover.	**número impar** número entero que siempre tiene el dígito 1, 3, 5, 7, o 9 en a posición de las unidades. Un número impar de objetos no puede ordenarse en pares o en dos grupos iguales sin que queden sobrantes.	21, 23, 25, 27, and 29 are odd numbers.
one fourth one of four equal parts of a whole.	**un cuarto** una de las cuatro partes iguales de un entero.	 4 equal parts
one half one of two equal parts of a whole.	**un medio** una de las dos partes iguales de un entero.	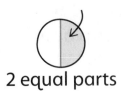 2 equal parts
one third one of three equal parts of a whole.	**un tercio** una de las tres partes iguales de un entero.	 3 equal parts

English	Español	Example/Ejemplo
ones single units or objects.	**unidades** elementos u objetos individuales.	 5 ones
open number line a straight line with only the numbers important to a problem labeled.	**recta numérica vacía** recta numérica que solo muestra los números que son importantes para el problema.	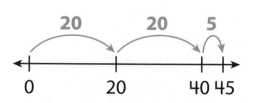

Pp

English	Español	Example/Ejemplo
penny a coin with a value of 1 cent (1¢).	**moneda de 1¢** moneda con un valor de 1 centavo (1¢).	 1 cent 1¢
pentagon a two-dimensional closed shape with exactly 5 sides and 5 angles.	**pentágono** figura bidimensional cerrada que tiene exactamente 5 lados y 5 ángulos.	
picture graph a data display in which pictures are used to show data.	**pictografía** representación de datos en la cual se usan dibujos para mostrar datos.	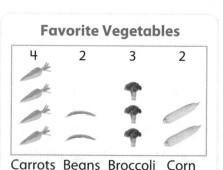 Favorite Vegetables

English	Español	Example/Ejemplo
place value the value assigned to a digit based on its position in a number. For example, the 2 in 324 is in the tens place and has a value of 2 tens, or 20.	**valor posicional** valor de un dígito según su posición en un número. Por ejemplo, el número 2 de 324 está en el lugar de las decenas; entonces, tiene un valor de 2 decenas, o 20.	 300 20 4
PM (or p.m.) the time from noon until before midnight.	**p. m.** tiempo desde el mediodía hasta la medianoche.	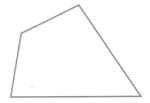

Qq

English	Español	Example/Ejemplo
quadrilateral a two-dimensional closed shape with exactly 4 sides and 4 angles.	**cuadrilátero** figura bidimensional cerrada que tiene exactamente 4 lados y 4 ángulos.	
quarter a coin with a value of 25 cents (25¢).	**moneda de 25¢** moneda con un valor de 25 centavos (25¢).	 25 cents 25¢

Rr

English	Español	Example/Ejemplo
rectangle a quadrilateral with 4 square corners. Opposite sides of a rectangle have the same length.	**rectángulo** cuadrilátero con 4 esquinas cuadradas. Los lados opuestos de un rectángulo tienen la misma longitud.	

English	Español	Example/Ejemplo
regroup to put together or break apart ones, tens, or hundreds.	**reagrupar** unir o separar unidades, decenas, o centenas.	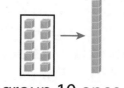 Regroup 10 ones as 1 ten
rhombus a quadrilateral with all sides the same length.	**rombo** cuadrilátero cuyos lados tienen todos la misma longitud.	
row a side-by-side (horizontal) line of objects or numbers, such as in an array or table.	**fila** línea horizontal de objetos o números, tal como las que aparecen en una matriz o una tabla. Los objetos o los números están uno al lado del otro.	
ruler a measuring stick that is marked in inches and centimeters. It shows 12 inches and 30 centimeters.	**regla** vara que tiene marcas que muestran pulgadas y centímetros. Muestra 12 pulgadas y 30 centímetros.	 Ruler shown is not life-size.

English	Español	Example/Ejemplo
Ss		

second (s)
a unit of time. There are 60 seconds in 1 minute.

segundo (s)
unidad de tiempo. 60 segundos equivalen a 1 minuto.

60 seconds = 1 minute

---

shorter
having a length or height that is less than that of another object.

más bajo
que tiene una altura menor que la de otro objeto.
más corto
que tiene una longitud menor que la de otro objeto.

← shorter

---

side
a line segment that forms part of a two-dimensional shape.

lado
segmento de recta que forma parte de una figura bidimensional.

side

---

skip-count
count by a number other than ones, such as count by twos, fives, tens, or hundreds.

contar salteado
no contar de uno en uno, sino de otra forma, como de 2 en 2, de 5 en 5, de 10 en 10, y de 100 en 100.

Skip-count by twos:
2, 4, 6, 8

---

square
a quadrilateral with 4 square corners and 4 sides of equal length.

cuadrado
cuadrilátero que tiene 4 esquinas cuadradas y 4 lados de igual longitud.

English	Español	Example/Ejemplo
subtract to take from, take apart, or compare to find the difference.	**restar** quitar, separar, o comparar para hallar la diferencia.	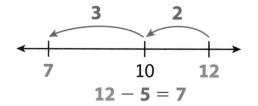 $12 - 5 = 7$
sum the result of addition.	**suma** el resultado de la suma.	$34 + 25 = 59$

Tt

English	Español	Example/Ejemplo
taller having a height that is greater than that of another object.	**más alto** que tiene una altura mayor que la de otro objeto.	 ← taller
tens groups of 10 ones.	**decenas** grupos de 10 unidades.	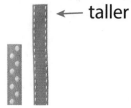 3 tens
thirds the parts formed when a whole is divided into three equal parts.	**tercios** partes que se forman cuando se divide un entero en tres partes iguales.	 3 equal parts

English	Español	Example/Ejemplo
trapezoid (exclusive) a quadrilateral with exactly one pair of parallel sides.	**trapecio** cuadrilátero que tiene exactamente un par de lados paralelos.	
trapezoid (inclusive) a quadrilateral with at least one pair of parallel sides.	**trapecio** cuadrilátero que tiene al menos un par de lados paralelos.	
triangle a two-dimensional closed shape with exactly 3 sides and 3 angles.	**triángulo** figura bidimensional cerrada con exactamente 3 lados y 3 ángulos.	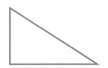

Uu

unknown number a number that is missing or not known in a problem, and is often shown as a box or a symbol.	**número desconocido** número que falta o que no se conoce en una ecuación que a veces se representa con una caja o un símbolo.	$18 - \;? = 9$ ↑ unknown number

Vv

vertex the point where two rays, lines, or line segments meet to form an angle.	**vértice** punto donde dos semirrectas, rectas o segmentos de recta se unen y forman un ángulo.	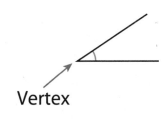 Vertex

English	Español	Example/Ejemplo

Yy

yard (yd)
a unit of length. There are 3 feet, or 36 inches, in 1 yard.

yarda (yd)
unidad de longitud. 1 yarda es igual a 3 pies o a 36 pulgadas.

3 feet = 1 yard
36 inches = 1 yard

yardstick
a measuring stick that is 1 yard long and shows 36 inches.

regla de 1 yarda
una regla que mide 1 yarda de longitud y muestra 36 pulgadas.

Acknowledgments

Common Core State Standards © 2010. National Governors Association Center for Best Practices and Council of Chief State School Officers. All rights reserved.

Photography Credits

United States coin images (unless otherwise indicated) from the United States Mint

Images used under license from **Shutterstock.com**.

iii Ahturner; **iv** Pavlo_K, Seth Gallmeyer; **v** Bubbers BB, David Franklin; **vi** Take Photo, Viktor Kunz; **vii** Butterfly Hunter, Galina Petrova; **1** Ajintai; **4** Prostock-studio; **5** kithanet; **6** Joey Chung; **8** Inna Astakhova, Aluna1; **9–10** Natalia D.; **12** Mike Flippo; **15** Andy Piatt; **16** Hayati Kayhan; **17** easyshutter, Lano4ka; **18** Stephanie Frey; **19** Crackerclips Stock Media; **20** Tamara Kulikova, Lalahouse; **22** Sergiy Kuzmin, Tiwat K; **25** Jiri Hera; **27** Noel Powell, blue67design; **28** mihalec, En min Shen; **29** catwalker; **30** Denis Burdin, Alex Alekseev, DR Travel Photo and Video, Hanna Kh, In-Finity; **32** BIGANDT.COM, Elisa Putti, Mary Rice, Alena Stalmashonak; **33** Oksana Kuzmina; **34** Picsfive; **36** Oksana Kuzmina; **39** Eric Isselee; **40** Steve Oehlenschlager, serazetdinov; **44** timquo; **45** Vasily Menshov; **47** bajinda; **49** onair; **51** Tim UR; **52** Sascha Burkard; **53** Peter Zijlstra; **54** Sailorr; **56** maxpro; **57** Matimix, liskus; **58** karn684; **60** Nadiia Korol, RioAbajoRio; **61** Elena Blokhina; **62** Dirk Ercken, artnLera; **63–64** Karkas, karn684; **66** Mygate; **67** Vyaseleva Elena, primiaou, artnLera; **69** Tom Biegalski, Lano4ka, Iriskana; **70** fivespots, blue67design; **71** De2marco; **72** Dionisvera; **73** Dudarev Mikhail, Iriskana; **75** Mauro Rodrigues; **76** AllNikArt, David Crockett; **77** Artem Kutsenko, Kyselova Inna, Nataly Studio, Nik Merkulov, Valentyn Volkov; **78** Fotofermer; **80** Maks Narodenko, Nataliia K, Oleksii Biriukov, Tim UR, Valentina Proskurina; **81** kp photograph, lasha, Mtsaride, pukach; **82** kp photograph, lasha, Mtsaride, pukach; **83** Jirateep sankote; **84** Hans Geel, marssanya; **86** Ivaylo Ivanov, Nataliia K, Oleksii Biriukov, Roman Samokhin; **87** Anton-Burakov; **88** Aluna1, iris wright; **89** Oleksii Biriukov; **91** Leigh Prather; **92** LAURA_VN, Olga_Angelloz; **93** Magic Pasta, RFvectors, VanReeel, vectorlight; **95** aksenova_yu, ALEX S, Magic Pasta, OGdesign, vectorlight; **98** Stanisic Vladimir; **99** Hawk777, Olga_Angelloz; **100** Lu Mikhaylova; **101** Africa Studio, NYS; **102** GalapagosPhoto; **104** KK Tan; **105** 5 second Studio; **106** Fafarumba, Roman Samokhin; **108** G_B_R_Jo, Kletr; **109** Pavel Hlystov; **110** Mega Pixel; **111** Looker_Studio; **112** Ahturner, runLenarun; **114** John T Takai, Yuri Samsonov; **115** Alexlukin; **116** JK's Design, lineartestpilot, Tsekhmister; **117** Hung Chung Chih; **118** Astarina, Cosma; **119** Steve Oehlenschlager, Yoko Design; **121** advent, Gopause; **123** Dakalova Iuliia; **124** Stuar; **126** Kirill Makarov; **128** Cameilia; **137** Lerner Vadim; **141** Arunas Gabalis; **144** absolut; **145** urbanbuzz; **146** AVS-Images, Lemonade Serenade; **148** Jantana, Nadiia Korol; **151** marssanya, Regien Paassen; **154** Aluna1, Kak2s, Tiwat K; **156** Low Sugar; **157** Olga Miltsova; **160** margouillat photo, runLenarun; **163** Ksuxa-muxa, nimon; **164** Dora Zett, blue67design; **165** Africa Studio; **166** ivansekretov; **168** Photosync; **169** Jiri Pavlik, Natasha Pankina; **172** catwalker; **174** Shebeko, smilewithjul; **175** Billion Photos; **177** Maryna Kulchytska, Natasha Pankina; **178** Alabass27; **181** Kyselova Inna; **185** Tamara Kulikova; **187** Marques; **188** Nik Merkulov; **189** Tatiana Popova; **190** threeseven; **192** Armari36, blue67design; **193** marilyn barbone; **196** Liskus, Ziben; **198** DR Travel Photo and Video; **199** Tyler Olson; **202** Tim UR; **203** ZoranOrcik; **206** Carolyn Franks, redchocolate; **207** Dan Thornberg, sirtravelalot;

209 Gyvafoto, Visual Generation; **211** Tamara Kulikova; **212** En min Shen; **213** Photo Melon; **216** Jenny Schuck; **218** I AM NIKOM; **220** Saltodemata, smilewithjul; **221** Blue67design, Mirko Rosenau; **223** marssanya, science photo; **224** Twin Design; **226** marssanya, Scanrail1; **227** ProStockStudio; **228** Kaspri, marssanya, smilewithjul; **229** Linda Vostrovska; **230** Nattika; **234** Elena Butinova; **236** mtphoto19; **239** Africa Studio, Eric Isselee, Natasha Pankina; **240** photastic; **241** Danza; **246** Chones; **249** Natalia Klenova; **250** Chones; **251** Africa Studio; **254** Carolyn Franks; **259** Elena Elisseeva; **260** Neamov; **262** Seth Gallmeyer; **263** RomGams; **264** FabrikaSimf; **271** Pavlo_K; **273** MyImages – Micha; **276** Happy Together, Yoko Design; **277** Johann Helgason; **286** Evastudio; **287** Africa Studio; **289** Christian Jung; **290** Zaretska Olga; **292** Ehtesham; **294** Jag_cz, David M. Schrader; **295** Tamara Kulikova; **296** Super Prin; **297** Eric Isselee; **303** SuriyaPhoto; **306** Cyril Hou; **316** Michael Drager; **318** Big and Serious, Daria Chichkareva, Jagodka; **319–320** Linett; **322** Nikolaeva, rangizzz; **326** kao; **328** CaseyMartin; **329–330** nfsphoto; **332** aperturesound; **333** Nata-Lia, Tulpahn; **334** graja, Sapunkele; **335** oksana2010, Popartic; **341** Dudarev Mikhail; **342** Bjphotographs, HstrongART, MITstudio; **346** Bubbers BB; **347** Brian A Jackson; **348** Robyn Mackenzie; **350** Rose Carson; **352** nanantachoke; **353–354** Ragnarock; **356** James Watts; **359** Africa Studio; **363** NikoNomad; **365** elbud; **366** En min Shen, junjun; **367** macondo; **370** Iriskana, tkemot; **377** MNI; **378** blue67design, timquo; **380** P Maxwell Photography; **381** eAlisa; **382** catwalker; **384** Marc Ward; **386** Petlia Roman; **387** blue67design, tarapong srichaiyos; **389–390** ChristianChan; **391** Denis Tabler; **392** Hamizan Yusof; **394** Eric Isselee, olnik_y; **395** Marijus Auruskevicius; **396** Natasha Pankina, wawritto; **398** puttsk; **400** HardheadMonster; **401** Olga Miltsova; **402** Sebastian Janicki; **408** ArtCookStudio; **409** Artush; **412** Sergey Ash; **413** NathalieB; **414** Ksander; **415** BIGANDT.COM, Elisa Putti, Smit; **416** belizar; **418** PHOTOCREO Michal Bednarek, foto-select, Vladimir Wrangel; **419** Jiangdi; **420** Niethammer Zoltan; **422** neftali, Oldrich, Zvonimir Atletic; **425** Billion Photos; **430** Lertsakwiman; **431** smilewithjul, Tamara Kulikova; **432** Tadeusz Wejkszo; **434** Kyselova Inna, smilewithjul; **435** Kim Reinick; **436** stockcreations, topform; **439** OtmarW; **440** Natalia D.; **442** opicobello; **443** Ljupco Smokovski; **446** Deyan Georgiev; **449** Studio DMM Photography, Designs & Art; **450** David Franklin; **453** Horatiu Bota, topform; **459** Kyrylo Glivin; **462** Chones; **463** Olga Reznik; **466** Rachel Brunette; **467** timquo; **468** lineartestpilot, timquo; **470** Ronnie Chua; **472** Steve Cukrov; **473** Tudor Ardeleanu; **474** garmoncheg; **475** Hurst Photo; **476** Mikhail Abramov; **477** Scanrail1; **479** Kthaikla; **480** Shaynepplstockphoto; **482** Jiri Hera; **484** Sandra van der Steen; **486** Sebra; **487** Africa Studio; **493** Roman Stetsyk; **497** Mizkit; **498** Matthias G. Ziegler; **500** Vitaly Zorkin; **501–502** Picsfive, M Kunz; **504** IB Photography, Yellow Cat; **505** Yellow Cat; **506** Sonia Dubois, Vitaly Zorkin; **507** xpixel; **508** ilovezion, Mizkit;

Front Cover Credits

©Auscape International Pty Ltd/Alamy
©Lynne Nicholson/Shutterstock

Illustration Credits

All Illustrations by **Tim Chi Ly**

510 NARUDON ATSAWALARPSAKUN; 511 Polina Prokofieva, MaraZe, Bragin Alexey; 512 Silvano audisio; 513 Yanas; 514 aperturesound; 515 Vladvm; 516 gresei; 518 Seregam; 519 Montego; 520 Wk1003mike; 522 MustafaNC, Belinda Pretorius, Dean bertoncelj; 523 Pictureguy; 524 Vadim Orlov, P Maxwell Photography; 526 Nerthuz, kontur-vid; 527 freesoulproduction; 528 Feng Yu, gillmar, Oliver Hoffman; 531 Mega Pixel, Tuomas Lehtinen; 532 Fedorov Oleksiy, Rawpixel.com, Polryaz; 535 timquo, Viktar Ramanenka; 536 Alhovik, Nik Merkulov; 537 Dan Kosmayer; 538 Marko Poplasen; 539 aopsan; 542 Roman Samokhin; 543 domnitsky; 544 Mega Pixel, koosen, Lunatictm; 545 PK.Phuket studio; 547 Ivonne Wierink, primiaou; 548 Tatiana Shepeleva; 549 Atlaspix, Mtlapcevic, drpnncpptak; 550 MyImages – Micha, Oleksandr Fediuk, Peter Vanco; 551 Blackspring; 552 Alexander Tolstykh, claire norman, Lufter; 553 Liam1949, Stockforlife; 554 Stepan Bormotov; 558 gillmar, Louella938; 559 Koosen; 560 Kamenetskiy Konstantin, Soonios Pro; 561 Sergiy Kuzmin; 564 Dora Zett, Verbitsky Denis; 566 Val Lawless; 568 Anton Starikov; 569 Photo One; 570 Picsfive; 572 Nor Gal, 573 Bulbspark, Nikola Bilic; 574 An NGUYEN, bulbspark; 576 Marish; 577 Vvoe; 578 Elena100; 581 endeavor; 582 NARUDON ATSAWALARPSAKUN, ULKASTUDIO; 584 RimmaOrphey; 585 StepanPopov; 586 Rakimm; 589 Exopixel, Pavel Bobrovskiy; 591 Coprid; 592 Godsend, Rashevskyi Viacheslav; 593 Peyker 594 Seregam, Peyker; 596 Ton Bangkeaw; 597 Arina P Habich; 598 reiza, Tarzhanova, Arina P Habich; 600 Mtsaride; 601 Irin-k; 602 oksana2010; 603 goi; 606 Arthito, mhatzapa; 607 Ivonne Wierink; 608 Picsfive; 609 viviamo; 611 FabrikaSimf; 612 Nik Merkulov; 613 Kitch Bain; 614 Nbenbow, schab; 616 Skobrik; 621 motorolka; 624 Solutioning Incorporated; 626 Ruslan Ivantsov; 629 Vahe 3D; 630 goodwin_x, Paleka; 634 Mhatzapa, Steve Oehlenschlager; 636 Scruggelgreen; 639 ang intaravichian; 640 Olha Ukhal; 642 Ton Bangkeaw;

644 MirasWonderland, ingret, Ermolaev Alexander, Oleksandr Lytvynenko, Eric Isselee, Dora Zett, Africa Studio, Olhastock, Grigorita Ko; 645 Eric Isselee, Laralova; 646 Alhovik; 648 BOONCHUAY PROMJIAM; 650 feelphoto2521; 651 stockfotoart; 653 Garsya; 654 Africa Studio, Picsfive; 655 azure1; 656 Sharon Silverman Boyd, Garsya; 658 Photka; 659 Rakic; 660 timquo; 661 Yaroslava; 664 Enrique Ramos; 666 Coprid, Lucie Lang; 668 valkoinen, timquo, iMoved Studio, grey_and; 669 Prasolov Alexei; 670 Africa Studio, Timquo; 671 Timquo, Pelfophoto, Airdone; 672 Vitaly Zorkin, Yellow Cat; 679 Alexandra Lande; 681 Galina Petrova; 682 Richard Griffin, indaflesh; 687 Elena Schweitzer; 688 Butterfly Hunter, SAPhotog, artshock, Handies Peak, Elena Schweitzer; 700 Oakozhan; 706 Andrey Eremin, Bigacis; 714 Izlan Somai; 716 kaspan, Mikhail Abramov, Africa Studio, Mamuka Gotsiridze; 717 Ruslan Grumble; alexmak7; 718 MNI; 722 Ravipat; 724 Rattanamanee Patpong; 732 Timquo; 733 GRSI; 736 Phovoir, Pumidol; 737 Chuckstock, Pixfiction; 740 Cherdchai charasri, freestyle images; 741 ajt, Ariadna Nevskaya, Marish; 744 Narong Jongsirikul; 745 Artem Kutsenk; 746 TukkataMoji; 747 Studio DMM Photography, Designs & Art; 749 Africa Studio; 751 Su Xingmin; 753 Aliaksei Tarasau; 754 Aperture51; 755 valkoinen; 758 kustome; 759 Mtsaride, FocusStocker, olnik_y; 762 Eric Isselee, Rudmer Zwerver, BlackAkaliko; 764 Zadiraka Evgenii; 765 Preto Perola; 766 Alan Lucas; 770 Dora Zett; 771 Africa Studio; 774 Stockforlife; 776 Suradech Prapairat, Stockforlife; 779 Mega Pixel; 780 Narong Jongsirikul; A4 titelio, Jiri Vaclavek, kitzcorner; A8 DenisNata; A9 Picsfive, Pogonici; A15 Picsfive; A16 Sasimoto

Student Handbook, appearing in Student Bookshelf and Teacher Guide only: HBi ArtMari, Pixfiction, Rawpixel.com, Disavorabuth; **HB1** Africa Studio; **HB2** iadams; **HB3** Palabra; **HB5** Havepino; **HB6** Tatiana Popova; **HB8** Chiyacat; **HB9** Kyselova Inna, Markus Mainka; **HB10** ArtMari; **HB11-HB12** ArtMari, Disavorabuth; **HB13-HB14** ArtMari; **HB18** Rawpixel.com